Grace in Time

Grace
in Time

A Memoir of Hope, Healing,
and Being Spared

Robert W. Finertie

ISBN: 978-1-7325988-8-1
E-ISBN: 978-1-7325988-9-8
Library of Congress Control Number: 2022918971

Cover and interior design by Tabitha Lahr

Printed in the United States of America

*This book is dedicated to anyone who has
ever been diagnosed with melanoma.*

Contents

Prologue

In December of 1976, I lay shivering on a stainless steel gurney in the hallway deep within the bowels of M.D. Anderson Hospital in Houston, Texas. Outside, the temperature was 98 degrees. Inside, the air conditioner cranked out frigid air. I longed for a blanket. I was alone and had been for a long time—four hours and thirty minutes by the wall clock—while the medical team planned what to do next. There were many possible outcomes in this war against melanoma. I knew this for a fact because my doctor had told me that they were considering amputating my leg.

The cold caused part of my shaking, but most of it was fear. I didn't want an amputation. But how could I not think about it? My mind turned toward the future. What would it be like to go through life like that? My mind drifted back to my youth: riding a bicycle, roller skating, jumping. Every memory was of my sturdy, capable legs that had served me well all these years. Recent memories surfaced. I loved kicker dancing, the waltz, and the Texas two-step. How would I do the two-step with one leg?

These questions bounced around in my head like Ping-Pong balls in the lottery selection. I focused on the past, fantasized about the future, anywhere but here and now, which was too painful a place to dwell. I depleted all my resources trying to be a tough guy, sucking it up, and willing myself to believe that everything was going to be okay. Now, at the end of my tether, I prayed, "God, I can't do this any longer. Please help me." After a brief silence, like the space that separates lightning from thunder, this message entered my mind: "*Thou dost keep in perfect peace the one who focuses his mind on Thee.*" After a short interval, another thought appeared: "*The Eternal God is your refuge, and underneath are the everlasting arms.*"

The Ping-Pong balls, so noisy and insistent only moments earlier, quieted. A profound sense of inner peace took their place, as well as the sensation that someone was carrying me, as when Dad scooped me up in his arms, cradled me up the stairs, put me in bed, and tucked me in. A power greater than myself, whom I call God, answered my prayer. A transcendent presence joined me in my struggle for existence in ways I could describe but not explain.

Chapter 1

Discovery

....

Fifteen months earlier, September 1975

My friend Jack and I had just finished a round of tennis. We were sweaty and thirsty and had come inside the clubhouse to cool off. After relaxing a bit with a Lone Star beer, Jack leaned in and said, "Bob, I have a friend who's a dermatologist. I'd like him to look at that dark spot on your leg." His comment took me by surprise. His knitted brow and general expression communicated concern, and his compassion popped my bubble of denial. I tried to discount his comment and pass it off as nothing, but Jack didn't buy it.

"Here's his number," he insisted, handing me a card. "I'll alert him that you'll be giving him a call."

I had also been a little concerned about that dark spot on my right leg just below the knee. At first, I thought a tick had bitten me and burrowed under my skin. When

I examined the area more closely, however, it wasn't hard or brittle like the body of a tick. I had wondered about it but not enough to form a plan of action. Jack's insistence got my attention and stirred a sense of urgency. I might as well have his friend examine me and give a professional opinion. The next day I called and set an appointment for the following week.

On the day of the appointment, I arrived early to fill out the paperwork. The nurse called my name and showed me into one of the examining rooms. While waiting, I studied the doctor's credentials hanging on the wall in matching frames. Scott Duncan had graduated pre-med from the University of Texas Southwest Medical Center in Dallas, and specialty training in dermatology at the Mayo Clinic. I felt reassured, knowing that whatever he needed to do, I would be in good hands. I didn't know what to expect, since this was all new to me. It didn't seem like anything to lose sleep over, but Jack's concern disturbed my nonchalance. My default defense mechanism leans more toward denial than hysteria, so I operate with a wait-and-see mentality. Tell me the facts. Don't sugar-coat them and don't lie to me. Give me the truth, and I'll find a way to deal with it.

Dr. Duncan knocked lightly on the door and entered the room. I liked him immediately. His eye contact, direct and caring, put me at ease. About my size and weight—six-one, 205 pounds—he wore gold-rimmed glasses, had a tan from the golf course or the beach, and appeared young, maybe in his mid-thirties. He carried himself with an air of confidence that helped quiet some of my anxiety.

He asked to see the dark spot, so I pulled up my pant leg, took off my shoe and stocking, and put my foot up on a stepstool. "This does look suspicious," he said. "I'll need to do a biopsy and send it to the pathology lab for examination." Wham. "Biopsy" triggered terror. Hit me like a punch to the solar plexus.

Dr. Duncan asked me to remove my pants and sit on the examination table. The paper crinkled beneath me. He numbed the area with a few injections around the site and left the room for a few minutes to allow the lidocaine to soak in. It also allowed the seriousness of this moment to soak in and twist my gut. When he came back into the room, I was surprised to see him holding what looked like a razor blade between his thumb and forefinger bent in the shape of a U. Picking up on my curiosity, he said, "It's called a double-edged blade. We've found that we get a cleaner cut this way, and the wound heals faster."

"Oh."

I felt disembodied, as though I were watching him operate on someone else. I saw the blade cutting into my skin and didn't feel any pain. I was grateful for the anesthetic. I studied his face as he cut, admiring his steadiness and his skill. Then his eyes narrowed to slits. His concern was unmistakable. The dark spot was about the size of a dime. In my mind, I imagined that he'd scoop it out like my mom used to scoop the eyes out of a potato before putting them into the pot to boil. What appeared to be a surface lesion went much deeper. Dr. Duncan asked me to lie back on the table because he had more to do. He put down the razor blade, injected more lidocaine, and picked up a scalpel. As the knife cut deeper into my flesh, my gut began to knot. This biopsy was more extensive than I had expected. He placed the specimen in a container that his nurse held out to him. Then he sutured the wound and covered it with a bandage. "The lab will send me a report in a few days," he said. "I'll call you then."

ONE WEEK LATER, THE PHONE RANG. "Dr. Duncan would like to speak to you," a nurse informed me. "Just a moment, please." During those moments, waiting, my nervous system jumped to red alert, my heart pounding and my mouth dry. Often, when test results were negative, the nurse called to let you know. Hearing from Dr. Duncan himself meant the news was not good, and the tension in his voice confirmed it. "The results on your biopsy show that it's melanoma," he informed me. "I have made an appointment for you at M.D. Anderson Hospital in Houston to confirm the results. Here's the number. Please call them to let them know you're coming."

This wham to the solar plexus took my breath away. My lizard brain called for adrenaline to deal with this crisis. My first thought was, *Ask not for whom the bell tolls; it tolls for thee.* After that, I rationalized, *There's been some mistake here; they must have mixed up the samples.* I tried to protect myself from pain by seeking comfort in denial. I was thinking, *Okay, I'll travel to Houston for a second opinion. They will confirm that the lab in San Antonio has made a mistake.* If I had any questions at this point, fear chased them out of my consciousness. I was so full of anxiety my cortex wasn't working. I didn't know what to expect or what questions I needed to ask.

Later, I would know that when you have cancer, melanoma is the kind you don't want to have. Basal cell is manageable (less than 1 percent metastasizes); squamous cell presents more of a challenge (it likes to go deep) but is still treatable. My knowledge of skin cancers would expand down the road when basal cell and squamous cell growths erupted on my face, scalp, and legs. An incision here, some cryosurgery with liquid nitrogen, some bandages and Aquaphor, plus some time to heal. Not a problem. Melanoma, on the other hand, is a killer.

Chapter 2

It's Melanoma

I hadn't wanted to upset Lynn at work, so I waited until after supper to break the news. She gasped, and her eyes got wide as tears welled up. "That's a bummer. Where do we go from here?"

"Doctor Duncan has scheduled an appointment next Monday at M. D. Anderson in Houston for a second opinion. I hope you can get off work to drive over with me."

"You betcha; I'll ask tomorrow."

We got up early Monday to make the three-and-a-half-hour drive to Houston. My appointment with Doctor McMurtry was at two. His grip was firm as he shook my hand. He wore a pinstripe shirt with a monogram on the cuff just above his manicured hand. When he moved, I caught a whiff of his aftershave. Photographs of nature gave his office an outdoorsy feel, a welcome contrast to the clinical atmosphere of the hospital.

"It's my hobby," he said when he saw me admiring his work.

His work evoked a deep sigh of appreciation from me. "Keep on clicking," I said.

"Thanks, I've been looking at your labs," he said. "The tests confirm it's melanoma."

My heart sank, and my palms got sweaty. This was not what I wanted to hear. There had been no mistake at the lab in San Antonio. Fear and dread took over my body and disturbed my peace. How could I be so full of fear and yet feel so empty?

"I've scheduled you for surgery on Friday to remove that lesion from your leg. Does that work for you?"

I turned to Lynn and asked, "Do we have any plans this weekend, Honey?"

"We'll make room for this," she said, reassuring me with a smile. There was no need to risk breaking a leg rushing into surgery, but there was no time to waste, either, not with melanoma, so I signed the acknowledgment and consent forms.

IN THE MORNING, WE MET WITH Wendy, a nurse. The orchid on her desk and a photograph of her dog warmed the clinical setting. She wore tasteful clothing, carried herself with confidence, and performed her job in a professional way. She managed the paperwork and explained to patients what the doctor planned to do.

"Things are happening fast here. How are you doing?"

"I'm more scared than I've ever been in my life, but I'm wearing my tough-guy mask,"

At forty-two, I had faced a few challenges along the

way—a broken leg in high school, three difficult years at seminary, Cathy's health challenges in Yoder, and a miscarriage with our third child in Pittsburgh—but this diagnosis jumped to the top of the list of degree of difficulty.

"Almost everybody finds surgery daunting. Would you like me to ask the chaplain to visit?"

"Yes, please."

"We've learned that patients do better when they know in advance what's going to happen, so I'm going to go over the treatment plan and answer any questions you have."

"Thank you," I replied, exhaling with relief.

"First, Dr. McMurtry will perfuse your right leg. That means he'll tie off your leg at the crotch with a tourniquet to prevent any chemicals from entering your body. After making a small incision to access the femoral artery near the top of your thigh, he will hook you up to a heart-lung machine that will pump medicine all through your right leg to kill off the bad guys. Okay, so far?"

I nodded, but I felt sick to my stomach, and sweat beaded up on my brow. All this was unpleasant to hear. Part of me wanted to leave the room.

"Then he will move to the original site and excise the diseased tissue until he has clear margins. The chemicals will mop up the rest."

The image of being carved like a Thanksgiving turkey stirred up the jitters in my belly, but Wendy's compassionate walk-through helped to soften some of my fears and put me at ease.

"How are you doing?"

"I'm dreading all this."

9

"Most people feel that way. It's okay. We will admit you on Thursday afternoon at two o'clock. Your surgery will be on Friday at ten."

I nodded again.

"Any questions?"

"Yes. Can I have a stand-in?"

She smiled and put her hand on my forearm. "See you on Thursday."

"Honey, how about some lunch before you drive back to San Antonio? My treat."

"Sounds good, Bob, especially the treat part."

I turned into a little Italian restaurant where we ordered minestrone soup and a salad and compared notes about the meeting with Wendy.

"Things are moving faster than I want to go, Honey," I said. "I want to call a time-out and catch my breath."

"I hear that. I'm feeling rushed too. At the same time, we don't want to give those bad guys a head start. Cancer doesn't take a vacation, ya know."

She flashed a fake smile to reassure me, toyed with her food, and smoothed her hair as she spoke.

"You're preachin' to the choir. I wanna punch somebody."

"Your jaws look tight. Who are you mad at?"

"I'm not sure. Maybe God. Is it safe to be mad at God? What if God gets mad back?"

"Hmm . . . what are you angry about?"

"Wouldn't you be? Here I was just starting to get my life back together after the divorce from Cathy. I met you and looked forward to waking up again. Now this. I feel like I'm back at the shore in New Jersey. Just before a storm, the waves get big. They knock you down and tumble you like clothes in a washing machine. As soon as you regain your footing, along comes another wave to knock you off your feet. It's just one damned thing after another. Now, instead of enjoying our honeymoon, we're learning about melanoma and chemotherapy."

I was trying my best to please God, figuring out what God wanted me to do with my life, and nothing was working. My jaw tightened up a little more each day as I encountered new frustrations. This was a time in my life I described as a *rotten, rocky, shit-assed trail.*

Taking both my hands in hers, Lynn said, "I'm disappointed about that too, Honey, but this changes our priorities. I want you to get better."

Tears welled up when I saw how she loved me.

"I do, too. Why isn't God cooperating?"

Lynn had to get back to the portrait studio because it wouldn't run without her. She dropped me off at my friend David's house. I had taken him up on his offer to stay with him in Houston instead of driving back to San Antonio. My lower lip quivered as I watched her drive away.

ON TUESDAY, AUGUST 5, TWO DAYS before my procedure, David arranged for us to join him and some friends that evening in his home for a pre-op party. He ordered a lot of pizza, which we washed down with liberal amounts of beer. One of his friends brought brownies for dessert, my favorite treat. They looked mouth-watering, stacked on the compote with crust baked crispy and dusted with confectioner's sugar, smelling chocolaty right out of the oven. As I reached for one, Karen, the baker, cautioned me with a wink and a knowing look in her eyes that they were "funny" brownies.

"Go ahead, try one," she said, "I made them especially for you."

My first thought was, *Do I want to do this?* I didn't remember anything in the pre-op instructions that said, "No funny brownies."

I ate one, savoring the rich chocolate flavor and the chewy texture. Later, a warm sensation spread through my body, and with it I felt the tension draining away.

David walked over from the wet bar and said, "Sue, I think Bob likes your brownies."

"I'm glad."

Soon I was laughing at everything. Jokes I would normally have groaned at sent me into spasms of laughter. Good ones doubled me over and brought tears to my eyes. Those brownies introduced me to cannabis. I slept well that night.

I ENTERED THE HOSPITAL ON WEDNESDAY, August 6, 1975. The surgery was Thursday morning at ten o'clock. I awoke from the anesthesia Thursday afternoon to find bandages covering a soft cast up to the middle of my thigh, and an intravenous line dripping medication into the vein in my left wrist. The nurse had wrapped a heating pad around my ankle. When I asked about it, she said, "There was a leak during the procedure. We want to increase circulation to that area." The anesthesia had caused some fuzzy disorientation, but I didn't feel any pain.

The nurses took good care of me and responded to my calls. I didn't like the first few meals after surgery; they were bland, and I was given no options. On the third day, I felt better when I could choose what I wanted from the menu.

On Sunday, three days later, Dr. McMurtry came to examine the wound. As he removed the bandages, shock and surprise rippled through my body. What had begun as a dime-sized dark spot below my right knee had morphed into a nine-inch incision extending four inches above my knee and five inches below. Sixteen stitches closed the wound. My leg had swollen from the surgical trauma and looked like an overstuffed sausage. I wondered how long it would take to return to normal size. Black catgut stitches drew the skin so tight I couldn't bend my knee. How long would it be before I could squat again?

The wound was healing and free of infection. All other systems were working, so the doctor discharged me. I called Lynn with the good news and asked her to come for me. My apartment back at the Antonian had a hot tub, a perfect spot to soak, bend, and stretch the skin to rehabilitate my knee.

Chapter 3

Meeting Lynn

I had been single for four years since my divorce, dating a bit but nothing serious, cautious about setting myself up to be hurt again, determined to resolve some of the issues that had sabotaged my chances for a healthy relationship in the past. One of them was my ambivalence about intimacy. What I both wanted and feared the most was to be close to another human being, yet my chest tightened, my legs grew restless, and my belly quivered when I ventured into vulnerability.

One day in July of 1974, my children were visiting. They loved the water and wanted to swim. The pool and hot tub were two reasons I had moved into the Antonian Apartments, along with the extra room for the weekends my children stayed with me. We had been swimming and diving for underwater toys for more than two hours and were tired. I called for a time-out of the pool. Spaghetti sauce was simmering for supper. Becky wrapped a towel around herself, curled up under the shade of an umbrella, and fell asleep. While we were relaxing, an attractive blonde walked by and stretched out on a chaise beside the pool. We had seen each other around the complex on our way to the mailboxes or the ice machine. I thought, *I'd like to meet her,* so I noodled for an opening line. I'm no social butterfly. Shy by nature, I become less sure of myself in the company of attractive, intelligent women. I was the guy who couldn't wait for Sadie Hawkins Day when the girls asked the guys to dance.

After racking my brain, nothing charming or catchy came to me, so I decided to keep it simple, as we had been learning in salesmanship class. I sidled up to the chaise next to hers and asked, "Are you saving this one?"

"Just for you," she said.

Encouraged by her friendly response, I ventured, "I'm Bob."

She extended her hand with a big smile. "I'm Lynn, glad to meet you."

Her warmth and openness disarmed me and dispelled my fear of rejection. She could have told me to get lost right after my opening line, but she hadn't. She put down her book and faced me. Our conversation was easy, eye contact solid. It was not a love-at-first-sight encounter, but I was curious to know more.

"Great day to catch some rays," I said, spreading my towel on the chaise.

"I know. I love this San Antonio weather. I've been watching you play with your children. How old are they?"

"Carolyn is sixteen. We call her Sissy; Stewart is twelve, Meredith is seven, and Becky is five."

"Nice family. That little one, Becky, is cute as a button."

"Thank you. Most days, I'd agree, but not so much today. Earlier, Becky couldn't find the top of her bathing suit and refused to go into the pool without it. When she realized she wouldn't be able to swim, she threw herself on the bed, howling."

"I'm sorry. Did you find it? She has a top on now."

"No, but Sissy saved the day. If you look closely, you'll see that she *drew* that top on Becky's body with Magic Markers."

"What a great job. I wouldn't have noticed." She smiled at me.

Something about how she said sorry, "sore-ey" instead of "sahr-ry," like I was used to hearing, hinted she came from a different part of the country. She tilted her head as she listened. I felt an attraction to Lynn and sensed she liked me too.

"Where you from?" I asked.

"Minnesota. Detroit Lakes."

"Where's that?"

"It's over at the western border. St. Cloud is the nearest big city."

I hadn't heard of either place. Becky woke up and came running over. "Daddy, I'm hungry," she announced.

"I'll bet you are; you were playing hard. Let's go check on the spaghetti. Nice talking to you, Lynn. I hope to see you around."

I was reluctant to leave, wishing we had more time.

"I need to feed these kids and get them back to their mom."

"Glad to meet you too, Bob. Bye."

On Thursday, four days later, I'd been thinking about Lynn and wanting to ask her out. As I left my apartment to take some clothes to the cleaner, I ran into her.

"Hi, Bob." She flashed me that compelling smile.

"Hi, Lynn, I was just thinking about you."

She paused for a moment, then said, "I didn't know you lived *here*."

"I've been here since the first of July."

"I moved into one of the studios on the other side of this building in June, just after I got a job at Sears."

"What do you do there?"

"I'm the manager of the Portrait Studio. Come by sometime, and I'll show you around."

"I'd love to." Then I took a deep breath and worked up my courage to ask her out. "After the tour, I'd like to take you to lunch."

"Luby's Cafeteria is nearby. I eat there a lot."

"Great. If Thursday works, how about next week?"

"I'd love that. My lunch break is from one to two."

"It's a date. Glad we bumped into each other. Bye, Lynn."

On the way to my car, I thought, *How easy was that?* I'd been sweating about how to ask Lynn for a date, and it had fallen right into my lap.

Time dragged waiting for Thursday. I drove from my office to the North Star Mall, just off 410 with the two-story cowboy boots out front and got there in twenty minutes. Lynn greeted me as soon as I walked into the studio, "Good afternoon, sir, please have a seat. I'll be with you as soon as I finish with this customer."

I enjoyed the chance to see Lynn at work as a photographer. When she turned on her charm, the family she was shooting, parents and three kids, were bright-eyed and smiling for their pictures. She concluded with that family and told them when their photographs would be ready.

She signaled for me to wait a minute, disappeared into another room, and came out with a diminutive Latina in her late teens dressed in coordinated pastels that accented her raven hair. "Bob, this is Dana, my assistant."

"Hi, Dana, glad to meet you."

"Hi, Bob. Lynn's been telling me about you."

I felt pleasantly surprised to hear this. Blood rushed to my cheeks in mild embarrassment because I wanted it to be true.

"Dana, Bob and I are going to lunch. I'll be back by two."

THE AROMAS WELCOMED US AS WE walked through the door at Luby's, a local cafeteria. We picked up a tray and scanned the wide selection before us. Lynn's favorite was the chicken pot pie. I picked pot roast after the waiter confirmed that they cooked the meat until you could break it apart with a fork.

Our table was over by a window, away from the noise of the other diners.

"Where did you go to school, Lynn?"

"St. Cloud State," she replied. "It was close to home, only a couple of hours away."

"How about you?"

"I went to Maryville College, in East Tennessee, not far from Knoxville. But it wasn't close to home; I wanted to get away and try out my wings."

"Where did you grow up?" she asked.

"In Delanco, New Jersey, about thirty miles down the Delaware River from Trenton."

The conversation continued like this over our simple meals, and before I knew it, the hour was up, and I'd barely eaten half my food.

"I've enjoyed this," she said. "Maybe we'll do it again sometime."

Her comment triggered a smile I couldn't contain. "I'd like that."

THE FOLLOWING WEEKEND, DANA HAD Lynn over for tacos, and I was invited. Dana lived with her parents in a spacious house in Alamo Heights. We followed her into a living room that struck me as part museum and part antique store. Beveled mirrors reflected our images as we entered. A Persian carpet softened the marble floor. Classic artwork covered the walls, and Chippendale chairs and sofa filled the room with leather and brass tacks. It was a royal decor.

Lynn had told me Dana raised cockatiels, so I wanted to meet them. I expected birdcages, but there weren't any. "Where are your birds?" I asked. Dana pointed up. I followed her finger to a decorative strip of wood about a foot below the ceiling. Four brightly colored cockatiels perched there, looking down their beaks at us. They had to know we were in the room, but there was neither a turn of a head nor a flap of a wing to acknowledge our presence. So we turned our attention back to our conversation, chips, guacamole, and drinks. Dana knew Lynn liked beer, so she had iced a few Coronas.

"How long have you two worked together?" I asked.

" A little more than a year," Lynn replied. "Dana was already working at the studio when I arrived. She taught me the ropes."

"That's right," Dana replied, "but Lynn's the one who got the business humming. She's a wizard with the kids. Her magic makes them smile, and that sells pictures. When the parents come back to look at the photos, they buy the whole package." She laughed when she told me that Lynn fell in love with all the kids who came in for portraits.

"I saw that last Thursday when I came to get you for lunch." Lynn's face beamed as she heard our compliments, and Dana went to get some snacks for us.

As I snacked and talked, the cockatiels flew from their perch, circled, and landed on my shoulders. Wings flapped around my head and face. Lynn laughed and put her hands to her face as though she were holding a camera to take a picture. Dana blurted out, "What the—? I don't believe this. They never go to anyone but me."

I felt flattered. I'm sure my face was flushed. I had to stifle an adrenaline rush triggered by this unexpected visitation. I enjoyed the strange intimacy of little feet clinging to my shirt, poking through the cloth, touching my skin. I wasn't sure what to do. The landing startled me a bit, but the birds' presence felt like a compliment. I was happy they wanted to be close, so I embraced the moment that lasted until we got up to leave. In their company, I felt a touch of grace. God can bless us in surprising ways.

COUNTRY MUSIC CROWDS THE AIRWAVES in San Antonio. Willie Nelson, one of the biggest C&W stars, grew up in Texas. He started at Floore's Country Store in

Helotes, Texas, twenty-two miles west of San Antonio, and never forgot his roots. After making it big on the country-western scene, Willie returned to Floore's every Fourth of July to perform, his way of saying thank you. At Floore's, Lynn and I discovered we loved dancing to country music, and we were good together. Other couples often stopped and asked us to show them our steps. Many western tunes are waltzes, so they lend themselves to the Texas two-step.

Whenever the band played Willie's "Blue Eyes Crying in the Rain," we stopped whatever we were doing—eating, drinking, or talking—and got up to dance. When we learned about Willie's Fourth of July concert, we stood in line for tickets. This concert always sold out. We dressed up in our cowboy finest and went there for an evening of dancing. The two favorite drinks at Floore's were beer and tequila: five beers iced down in a galvanized bucket and a basket of tortilla chips and salsa; tequila in one-ounce shooters on demand. I learned to nurse a beer and leave the rest for Lynn. It was not a matter of moral rectitude but a simple truth; when I drank more than one, my legs stopped working and spoiled my dancing. So one beer for me and water after that.

IN TEXAS, DURING THE DOG DAYS OF August, the sun cooks the door handles of your car till they're too hot to touch. It overheats the roads and sidewalks till they burn your feet and sends the cows scrambling for shade under the live oak trees. People flee the cities and head south to Port Aransas on the Gulf Coast or northeast to Canyon Lake. Another way to escape the heat is to go tubing on the Guadalupe River. Horseshoe Bend calls out to people who love to be in the water.

Lynn and I drove to New Braunfels in forty-five minutes, rented some tubes—one for each of us and one to float the cooler—and found a place to park. We hiked the footpath to the put-in. The water is so cold it takes your breath away, so most people try to drop into their tubes without getting wet. Once you put your tube in the water, the current makes it a moving target. Only one person in ten can land in the center and remain upright. The rest bounce off or miss the tube entirely, ending up in the water. They surface yelling, coughing, and sputtering. Lynn and I solved the entry by facing away from the water, holding our tubes behind us, and falling backward.

Noisy is the norm at put-in as crowds of people get underway. Your body adjusts to the water temperature quickly and welcomes the change from the hundred-plus-degree air. Everybody brings beer, but sometimes newbies forget sunscreen, a mistake they won't make twice.

The crowd thins as the type A's hustle downstream, paddling like maniacs as though this were a race.

"Lynn, I'm not a fast-lane guy. Let's relax, and let the river do the work, OK?"

"You bet. We'll crack a couple of brewskis, kick back, and enjoy the ride."

At this point Lynn and I had known each other for two months. We'd had lunch at Luby's and tacos at Dana's. We'd been dancing at Floore's and tubing on the Guadalupe. We were getting to know each other and feeling comfortable to be ourselves around each other.

That settled, we paddled closer to the riverbank to savor the quiet and let the current ferry us through the extensive stands of cattails and elephant ears. After a few minutes, we drank a beer to cool down on the inside. The aroma of smoked brisket made us hungry as we floated past people grilling on the riverbank. An occasional cloud of blue smoke from cannabis made me want to breathe a little deeper. That smoke is as distinctive as a whiff of cigar or gasoline. Large flotillas of people holding their tubes together with their legs passed us by, loud and heedless of the beauty surrounding them. There are no houses along the riverbank, and I found peace in the quiet loveliness of the natural setting.

As we got to the end of the float, houses started to appear. "Look at all these houses, Honey. What a location."

"Maybe not. I wouldn't want these tubers in my backyard all summer."

"They must have built here early, before the city fathers passed zoning laws to forbid it."

The deep green foliage, the clarity of the water—you could see the bottom as you drifted—and the natural power of the current all joined to provide a relaxing way to beat the heat. The trip took an hour and a half and ranked high on our list of favorite activities. At the end of the first run, we took a bio break and got some chips at the country store.

"Want to go around again?" I asked.

"I do," she replied, "now that we've made that pit stop."

We carried our tubes back to the put-in and made a second loop. The draw of Horseshoe Bend was this: At the end of the float, you could walk about a quarter mile across the open end of the horseshoe and return to the put-in. This saved having to park a second car at the end to drive back to the beginning.

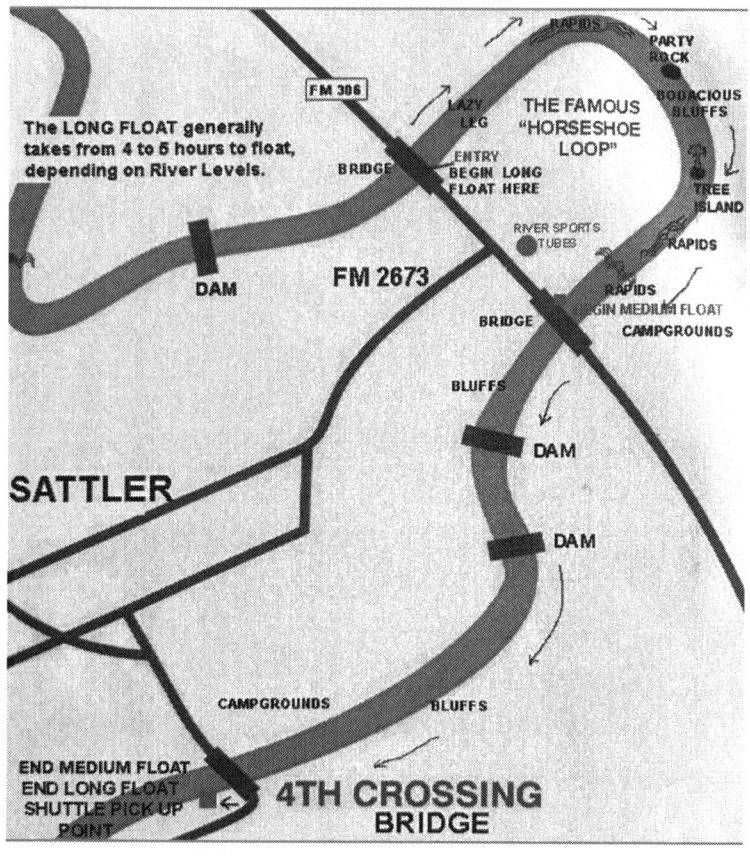

After that, we felt nuked by the sun, our muscles ached, and our tummies grumbled.

"Honey, I've had all the fun I can stand for one day. How about you?"

"Me too. I'm way too tired to cook, so why don't we stop for barbeque on the way home?"

"Great way to ice the cake."

JUST BEFORE CHRISTMAS, OUR relationship expanded and deepened when Lynn invited me to meet the rest of her family over the holiday. Lynn's father, Orvis, drove, and Lynn and I were passengers as we motored from San Antonio to her younger sister, Laurel's home in Dallas. Laurel and her husband, Jeff, hosted the event in their new house. Kay, the eldest, and her husband flew down from Chicago to join us. This extended family enjoyed being together and playing card games like hearts, spades, and bridge. The Olson family also loved to talk, and meals offered the perfect occasion. I had trouble getting a word in, so I listened a lot unless someone asked a question to draw me into the conversation. Inwardly I noticed the difference between this family and the one I'd grown up in, where silence prevailed, and tension triggered migraine headaches at holiday gatherings. Genuine sadness filed my heart when the holiday ended, because we had to break up this happy gathering and go home.

LYNN'S PARENTS, ORVIS AND GUDDY, motored south with the snowbirds as winter began in Detroit Lakes, Minnesota. They booked an extended stay at a New

Braunfels motel because of its proximity to the Landa Park Par-3 Golf Course. Orvis often boasted while out on the course, "I'd rather be playing golf than shovelin' snow like the folks back in Detroit Lakes are doing."

The par-3 genre fills a niche between putt-putt layouts and regulation country club and municipal courses. Golfers leave their woods and drivers home and play a par 3 with three clubs: a chipper (7 or 8 iron), a pitcher (sand wedge), and a putter. Players start with the ball on the ground. They want to be on the green in two and finish the hole with a putt. Par 3 offers a way to sharpen your short game: chipping, pitching, and putting. A chip shot rolls farther than it flies, while a pitch flies farther than it rolls. None of us was any good. We were duffers, inexperienced at golf, but we loved being out in the sunshine with grass underfoot, enjoying the rolling hills of Texas, the live oak trees, and the sounds of doves flying overhead.

One day we had played eight holes and were approaching the ninth, which offered a challenge. You had to pitch up about ten feet to get on the green. When I walked up to the flag, I saw that Orvis had made a great shot within two feet of the cup. He couldn't see his lie as he walked up to the green with his putter in hand. He couldn't see me either as I replaced his ball with a "trick" ball that wouldn't roll in a straight line. The rest of us were away, so we putted out and stood by to watch Orvis. All eyes were on him as he lined up his putt. His knitted brow revealed that he was trying to concentrate, but the grin from his great approach shot got in the way. He backed off for a few moments to gather himself for this crucial putt. When he struck the ball, it looked like a Mexican jumping bean, so erratic it never got within a foot of the hole. "What the heck happened," he said. Then he realized that someone had pranked him. He enjoyed playing tricks as much as any of us. He shook his head in disbelief at missing that "gimme," picked up his ball, and looked my way with a knowing smile. Afterward, the ninth hole never played the same, as memories of that magnificent miss intruded.

Chapter 4

Channels of Grace

....

W hen daffodils bloom, grass greens, and the limbs
of the trees sport fresh buds, we recognize these
things as harbingers of spring, a season of new begin-
nings. But spring can also be a time of endings. Spring of
1970 was one of those endings for me, a painful time of
grievous losses and heartbreaking sorrow. My marriage of
thirteen years was over. My career of ten years as a pastor
was gone. Before long, I would be leaving my friends
behind. The hole in my chest was as big as a basketball.
The pain felt like someone had run my heart through a
shredder. Strips of raw flesh hung down inside like the
blisters on the roof of my mouth when I eat pizza just
out of the oven before it has had a chance to cool. The
injuries from hot pizza heal in a week or two. Wounds
from divorce take a lot longer.

Confusion addled my mind. Three of my friends who
were also pastors had affairs; their wives forgave them,

their marriages survived, and they continued to serve as pastors. Two other fellow pastors were unfaithful and later committed suicide. I strayed from the straight and narrow, and my wife filed for divorce. The "why" question came up a lot. I never found an answer. The "what" question has proved far more helpful to me: *What* can I do now that this has happened? The "what" question has an answer that shows me the next step and helps me to keep moving forward, while "why?" keeps me focused on the past.

Here is how it happened. My wife, Cathy, and I were at the breakfast table one morning. We had been married for thirteen years and had four children. The kids had caught the bus and were on their way to school. I was clearing the dirty dishes from the table. The air was thick between us over financial issues we did not know how to resolve. But there was more. I had a crush on one of the members of my congregation, and it was tearing me apart. Whenever DJs played "Torn Between Two Lovers," I would start to cry. That song gave a voice to my dilemma, described the unspoken broken inside me. This dark secret was hanging ominously over our relationship. Cathy could feel the tension and wanted to clear the air, so she said, "What's wrong, Bob?"

"A lot of stress at work." That was the truth, but not all of it.

"I know something's wrong; I can sense it."

I squirmed and hesitated to reply, trying to weigh my answer, knowing that a lot was riding on it. Did I keep on blowing smoke, or did I come clean?

"Don't keep telling me nothing's wrong when I know there is. For God's sake, tell me what it is so we can work on it together. You've slept with her, haven't you?"

In my heart, I knew that sometime sooner or later, the truth would out. I thought this was an invitation to begin the process. It did not look like an invitation to go to hell. Sure fooled me. Soon after that, I experienced the "hell hath no fury" part.

THE DIVORCE WAS NOT COMPLICATED. No need to contest it. Not much to fight over. Our house was owned by the church. All we owned was the furniture inside and the cars we were driving. Earlier, a Mayflower van had driven away with the furniture Cathy wanted. I watched as a pickup left the driveway with a three-piece sofa, the last of the items that neither of us had room to keep. I could stay in the house for two months while I looked for work. After that, I would be moving too, destination unknown.

Cathy and the children were staying with friends during this awkward time. Cathy hatched a plan for me to be out of town with a friend while she and the children packed up their things and left. I would come home to an empty house without any chance to say goodbye. One of my friends found out about the plan and alerted me so I could be with them until they left. Stu, who was ten, asked if we could play catch as a way of breaking the tension. So I got a ball, and we went out in the front yard to wait for their ride to the airport. Sadness welled up inside me when the taxi stopped at the curb. I bear-hugged each of the children and felt my diaphragm trembling as I choked out, "I love you" and kissed them goodbye. Most of the people I loved just drove away without their dad. Not knowing when we would see each other again, I went inside the house, closed the door, and crumpled to

31

the floor. I was alone, feeling abandoned, just like when Mom died. I did not understand. I thought Cathy and I would work it out, but we couldn't. Now she was on her way to San Antonio, where her parents lived. In less than a nanosecond, I regressed to the earlier loss and tapped into that bottomless pool of unresolved sorrow, while a persistent question pinged in my mind: "Who's going to take care of me now?" A voice from somewhere said, "You are." I guess I had a lot of growing up to do.

THE TELEPHONE RANG AND STARTLED ME. I wondered who might be calling, friend or foe. I exhaled a huge sigh of relief when the voice at the other end said, "Hi, Bob, this is Bill Rentz (one of the elders from the church). Dot and I would like you to come over to the house. She's fixing supper. Bring your bathing suit." I ignored the non sequitur and didn't raise any questions.

"Thanks, Bill. I'll be there in ten minutes."

During the drive, I thought, *What a gracious offer and kindness for them to share their food and presence with me.*

Their house was big and sat high on a hill, the only home I have ever seen with an indoor swimming pool. Bill managed a team of twelve district supervisors whose job was to distribute the local papers to subscribers. As I walked through the entrance, I savored the teasing aroma of food cooking. "Boy, that smells good, Bill."

"Dot's fixing steaks, and she says it will be a while before supper. Let's jump into the pool until it's ready. Follow me." Condensation covered the glass on the door to the pool. The sharpness of the chlorine assaulted our nostrils; heat and humidity felt oppressive as we walked through the door. Bill grabbed a big beach ball from the toybox and tossed it in the water. He jumped into the pool after it, raising a geyser; a guy his size displaces a lot of water. We enjoyed hitting the ball back and forth, trying to see how many times we could keep it in the air. At first, we were clumsy. We hit the ball too hard or not hard enough or off to the side, so we had to start over after two or three hits. We got better over time, improving to ten hits, then twenty-five, then fifty. Before I moved away, we reached 123 times. We cracked a beer to celebrate. Dot called down, "Supper's ready."

While I was with Bill and Dot, it felt like I had stumbled into an oasis after a long journey in the desert. It was a time of rest and refreshment. They offered me a haven where I could relax and soak up their nurturing, the kind of place I had yearned for as a child. Their loving hospitality helped me to reengage with people. After the divorce, I was not sure who were the enemy and who were still my friends. This simple kindness of inviting me over to their home for dinner became an act of grace that stirred up hope in me. If Bill and Dot could love and forgive me, maybe I could learn to love and forgive myself, even if only a little.

Chapter 5

Finding Work

....

Even when the night is darkest and the storm at its worst, flashes of lightning illuminate the landscape. I could see one thing clearly: from this moment, I would no longer be a minister in the Presbyterian Church. Hot tears formed as I read in a letter from the presbytery that I had two choices: I could voluntarily demit the ministry (turn in my resignation), or I could submit to the formal discipline of defrocking in front of my peers. The degree of my self-hatred, which was intense at times, could not eclipse the level of masochism involved in the second option. I elected to resign. This action meant that I could no longer be a minister of the Word and Sacrament in the Presbyterian Church. Job offers (calls) to work at any church within the denomination would be declined by the presbytery because I would no longer be ordained.

My work as a pastor was over. I was not thrilled about that, but I was learning to accept it. I would need to look elsewhere. Harsh realities began to close in. Entry-level positions with Alcoa Aluminum and US Steel were available, but I rejected them; I was not that desperate yet. Over the next six weeks, I updated my resumé and took a barrage of aptitude tests. Several insurance companies showed an interest in me. "You have the aptitude," they said. From among those interested, I selected New York Life, a large, eastern mutual company that had been in business since 1845.

In August of 1971, two months after Cathy and the children moved out and after seven weeks of looking for a job, I rented a U-Haul trailer, packed my belongings in it, stopped to say goodbye to Bill and Dot, and headed north out of Pittsburgh to my new job in Buffalo, New York. I stayed with the Rev. Rocky Munson and his wife, Phyllis, for three weeks until I could find a place of my own. Rocky was a friend and pastor I had known in Pittsburgh. Their friend Audley McLean, an assistant manager at New York Life, would be my mentor in the new job. I found a flat to hang my hat on the second floor above the owners, a kindly Polish couple named Siudzinski.

To get to work, I drove the Scajaquada Expressway, and each morning I would put a smile on my face, call prospects, set appointments, make presentations, and close sales. That is the job description of a life insurance agent. After work, I would drive home, fix some supper, get ready for bed, and cry myself to sleep.

Selling insurance is hard, even when conditions are favorable; to begin a new career in a strange city where I knew only three people bordered on insanity. The challenge was to expand my circles of acquaintances as fast as possible. One morning I needed a break and a stretch, so I stepped out of the office and walked two blocks to a local coffee shop. Standing in line, I struck up a conversation with the guy in front of me. That's how I met John Doud.

John and I hit it off from the moment we met. He said, "I've got the coffee. Let's sit outside; it's such a gorgeous day." After we found a table, he asked, "What brings you to Buffalo?"

"A new job I heard about from a friend in Pittsburgh."

"What will you be doing?" he said, leaning forward as if he was eager to hear everything about me.

"Selling insurance with New York Life."

"Oh." (Usually, that meant *I'm not interested*, and the conversation ended, but not with John.) "That could be a challenge," he said, "especially when you've just moved here from another state and don't know many people."

"Touché. How about yourself, John? What do you do?" I asked, sipping my coffee.

"I work at the Suicide Prevention and Crisis Service Center a few blocks from here."

"That's interesting." I added, "I volunteered at the Suicide Prevention and Crisis Service Center when I lived in Pittsburgh."

"John," a voice said as a gentleman in clerical garb approached us.

"Good morning, Father. I want you to meet Bob Finertie. He just moved here from Pittsburgh."

"Hi, Bob, I'm Chad. I'm on staff at Trinity Episcopal Church, across the way."

"Chad's modest," John said. "He's actually the vicar."

"Glad to meet you, Vicar," I said, feeling blessed to be meeting such outstanding leaders of the community.

"Has John invited you to join our prayer group, Bob?"

"I was going to, Chad, but you beat me to the punch. That would be an ideal way for Bob to meet a few of the folks from Buffalo."

The vicar excused himself to attend a meeting, but John and I continued our conversation for more than an hour. I enjoyed getting to know more about my new friend—I liked his warmth and his caring nature. He seemed well-suited to his calling. John offered to drive if I wanted to meet with the prayer group, so I agreed. The group met on Tuesday evenings at six thirty and provided a place for people to voice their concerns and support one another.

At the first meeting in December, Ann shared problems she was facing at work, Ray asked for prayers around a health issue, and Melody expressed how inadequate she felt being a single mom. After that, Pam, the leader, turned to me and said, "Okay, Bob, it's your turn. How are things going?"

"Thank you for inviting me to your group. I was a stranger, and you took me in. I appreciate that."

"We're glad to have you in the group."

"What I'm struggling with tonight is how much I miss my children." I only got a few words out before all the sadness inside erupted, and I had trouble going on. I paused and took a couple of deep breaths to compose myself before continuing. "Especially with the holidays coming. I didn't get to see them at all last year. That was the loneliest Christmas of my life."

I heard various voices in the group say, "I'll bet it was . . . How awful . . . That's so sad."

"I've been working hard at my new job so I can support all of us. I don't mind the work, I can do that, but I struggle with the loneliness, coming home to an empty apartment, eating alone, and crying. I'm making enough sales to pay my bills. My boss says he's proud of me. On payday, the first check I write is to Cathy for child support. That's half of my earnings; the rest goes for my food, rent, and expenses. I miss my kids a lot and long to see them over the holidays." More tears and sobbing racked my body and interrupted my story, but I managed to go on. "There's nothing left in my budget for travel. A visit in person is the deepest yearning of my heart and my most unlikely fantasy."

I could see several in the group tearing up as they listened to my story. When the prayer meeting was over, we enjoyed a time of refreshments and socializing. John Brust, one of the members, eased up to me and said, "Bob, the way you shared about missing your children touched my heart. I could feel how much you long to see them. My wife, Elsie, and I talked about that and agreed that we would like to make that happen."

"Oh, John," I said, embarrassed by my tears. "Really? I can hardly believe what I'm hearing."

"Here's my business card." He smiled and urged his card into my hand. "Stop by my office in the morning, and I'll have something for you."

"I will, John, but right now, I'm speechless."

He grinned and said, "You'll get over it. Is nine o'clock, okay?"

"I'll be there."

I stood there, struggling to take in his generosity and welcoming manner. It was hard for me to receive from others, but at that moment, I sensed that it was God's grace helping me be in the right place.

The next day I arrived early, curious about this meeting. John greeted me with a smile and showed me into his office. "I've looked into the cost of a round trip to San Antonio. Inside this envelope is some money for you to visit your kids. It's a gift from Elsie and me. Merry Christmas."

"Oh, John," I said, struggling with emotion, "God bless you."

"He has," he said, "and we're passing some of those blessings along to you."

I thanked him again and left his office. Once outside, I opened the envelope and found a check for one thousand dollars made out to me. Tears of gratitude and joy stained that envelope.

OVER THE YEARS, I HAVE PONDERED the way my path has intersected with the lives of other people. Sometimes the circumstances have seemed far too complicated and intricate to be random or accidental, so I call them "divine appointments." Here I was in Buffalo, racked by more losses than my mind could process. I was as sad and depressed as I have ever been in my life. I was powerless and alone when I met John, and he introduced me to his vicar and the prayer group. I felt supported by the members as they listened to the challenges I was facing. I felt the strength and comfort of the group as we stood together in a circle. Power passed between us as we held hands and prayed. They came through for me in ways I had never imagined.

There were days when I wished I had less stress in my life. There were nights when I cried myself to sleep.

I prayed for my sadness to end. I prayed for the ache of separation from my children to stop. I did not pray for my life to end. Sometimes I wondered if God had John on standby, just in case.

AROUND THE SAME TIME I MET John Doud, I started attending the First Presbyterian Church in Tonawanda. Before long, I joined the choir where George Reed sang next to me in the bass section. George was a traveling salesman, and over time we became good friends. He and his wife, Doris, invited me to join them for dinner one Sunday following worship. Tossing a Frisbee around with their children in the back yard until it was time to eat put joy in my heart and a smile on my face. The exercise worked up an appetite for the delicious meal Doris prepared. After dinner we assembled in their game room to play war, dominoes, and Chinese checkers. Soon I was a regular visitor. They took me in and allowed God's grace to flow through them to me as a member of their extended family.

One day I asked George if he would listen to my sales presentation and offer feedback, since he was a salesman. He agreed. Afterward, he bought a $50,000 whole life policy. This sale was a feather in my cap and a significant boost toward meeting my sales goal for the month. Once we had completed the application, I asked George how he had gotten to be forty-eight years old, married with four children, and had never bought a stick of insurance. He said, "I never met a salesman I could trust."

In December, before I left to visit my children in San Antonio for the holidays, I contacted Eddie Johnston, the

New York Life general manager. I explained that I wanted to transfer to his office so I could be near my children. After looking over my production record in Buffalo, he said, "I can always use a good agent like you."

Chapter 6

Hoping for a Transfer

E very nerve ending in my body tingled with excitement in anticipation of seeing my children over the
holidays. The ticket in my briefcase would allow this to
happen, thanks to the generosity of the prayer group. In
my mind, I fantasized about our time together: the hugs
we'd share, our visit to the zoo, the pizza we'd wolf down
at Capparelli's Restaurant, and the joy of being with them.

This visit, which was mainly to spend time with my
children, would offer a perfect opportunity to meet with
the general manager of New York Life in San Antonio
to see if I might transfer there from Buffalo. It seemed
too good to be true.

I SAT IN THE RECEPTION AREA OF THE San Antonio
office on December 20, 1973, my jaws tight and my
stomach full of butterflies. Christmas loomed five days

away. I had flown here from Buffalo on the ticket John and Elsie Brust provided.

While I waited, I soaked in the ambiance: the warmth of the leather furniture on the backs of my legs, the deep pile carpeting under my feet, and the way the fabric wall covering softened the room. I noted the contrast between this office and the Department of Motor Vehicles where I renewed my driver's license. These creature comforts helped to ease some of the anxiety I felt about the meeting. A lot was riding on the outcome. If Mr. Johnston hired me, I could leave Buffalo's brutal winters behind and move to San Antonio. Warmer weather would be a welcome perk, but more than anything I wanted to be near my children. I had worked to keep in touch with phone calls, letters, and audio cassette tapes, but nothing beats a real live bearhug. I missed the four of them: Carolyn, fifteen, Stewart, twelve, Meredith, seven, and Becky, three. After their mother, Cathy, and I divorced in 1971, she moved to San Antonio to be near her parents, and I moved to Buffalo to start working for New York Life. I choked back tears, registering that a year and a half had passed since I'd seen them.

GRATITUDE FILLED MY MIND AS I remembered the support and encouragement of the prayer group back in Buffalo. Their generosity had funded this trip. The receptionist broke into my reverie, announcing, "Mr. Finertie, Mr. Johnston will see you now. This way, please."

"Mr. Johnston, Mr. Finertie."

Mr. Johnston flashed a welcoming smile as he lumbered out of his chair to greet me, surprisingly graceful for a big man. "Bob Finertie," he said. "Welcome to Texas."

His warmth filled the room and eased my discomfort. His move to a chair alongside me eliminated his desk as a barrier and made our interview more intimate.

"I've heard a lot of good things about you from your manager in Buffalo."

"Glad to hear," I said. "I've been working hard to get established up there."

"So, you'd like to transfer to the San Antonio general office."

"That's right. I showed I can sell insurance in Buffalo. I think I can do it here. Plus, if I'm living here, I can visit my children on weekends. I haven't seen my kids in a year and a half, and I miss them."

"I can appreciate that. I think it's fantastic that your first year as an agent was such a good one. Your manager up there tells me you won a trip to the home office in New York City."

"That's right. I met Vice President Hussey, who took me on a tour of the home office and gave me a plaque that I was proud to hang in my office when I got back to Buffalo."

"Great job, or, as they say in Texas, you done good."

"Thanks, Mr. Johnston."

"You can call me Eddie. I can always use a strong producer like you. I'm ready to hire you now. How soon can you move down here?"

"I'll have to talk to Frank, my manager in Buffalo, and let you know; probably sometime after the first of the year. Thank you so much, Eddie. I've enjoyed meeting you and look forward to working together. I'll be in touch."

"The pleasure was on this end. Enjoy this time with your kids and have a safe trip home. See you next year, Bob."

Chapter 7

Winter in Buffalo

....

Aſter visiting my children in San Antonio over
the Christmas holidays and arranging with Mr.
Johnston to transfer from Buffalo to San Antonio, I
returned to Buffalo to wrap up my work there, my spirits
buoyed by his warm welcome and job offer. I had been
toiling for a long time without any tangible rewards. Now
I felt encouraged that the tide was turning, and smoother
sailing lay ahead of me.

Arriving at the airport in Buffalo on my return after
Christmas, I looked out the window as the wheels touched
down and felt shocked and surprised to see the ground
covered with snow. It was still winter on January 5, 1973,
but when I left Buffalo, it had been balmy, so I'd worn a
polo shirt. I knew it would be warm in San Antonio and
packed accordingly, and I had no winter clothes in my
bag. However, the weather had changed while I was away,
and that reality quickly set in. At departure, it had been

sunny and warm; now it was freezing, and I had parked in a distant lot because of the holiday traffic. I rode the airport shuttle out to my car, and my heart sank when I saw it. Freezing rain had wrapped it in a blanket of ice and cemented the windshield wipers to the glass. When I turned the key in the lock, nothing happened. I tugged with all my strength, but the door wouldn't budge. It had frozen to the body of the car.

Panic rushed through my body as I considered my situation. I was locked out of my car, my teeth were chattering, and my body shivered from the freezing wind as I puzzled over what to do next.

The shuttle driver saw my plight and offered to take me back to the terminal for a bucket of warm water to melt the ice around the door. That accomplished, I climbed inside and put the key in the ignition with a silent *please start* prayer, wondering what else might go wrong. The car came to life at the first crank, and I could breathe again, knowing that the heat from the engine would soon defrost the windows, warm the cabin, and thaw me out. I discovered that *soon* is a relative term. If you're warm at the beginning, the process doesn't take long. But when your teeth are already chattering uncontrollably, it seems to take forever. Eventually, the windshield cleared, and the cabin warmed up, but my body kept shaking, and I worried about getting pneumonia.

I DROVE FROM THE AIRPORT TO MY second-story flat above the Siudzinskis', put on my sweats, and fixed a cup of tea. That winter of 1973 was one of the most challenging times I have ever faced. A few days later,

I caught the flu. The bug interfered with the regular operation of my top and bottom sphincters. Spouting from both ends only increased my misery. Whatever I ate either bounced back up or ran straight through me. I called Audley, my manager, to let him know I was taking a sick day. He stopped by the house around noon with some soup and crackers for lunch. I was unable to get far from the loo all day. Audley looked in again on his way home from work and brought burgers and fries, probably not the best fare for someone in digestive distress. My symptoms continued throughout the evening unabated. Around ten thirty, I heard a knock on the door. I wondered who would come calling so late. When I opened the door, it was Mr. Siudzinski, my landlord, in his pajamas, robe, and slippers, with a bottle of whiskey in one hand and a shot glass in the other.

"I brought you some medicine," he said as he filled the glass. "Drink that. It will help settle your stomach."

I felt like I might have to die to get better, but I did as he said.

"Here's another one," he said. "It will help you sleep." He did not add, "It will help us sleep too," but I'm sure he hoped it would.

"I'll leave one on the dresser for morning," he added as he left.

"Thank you," I croaked. I could not imagine drinking whiskey first thing in the morning, so I tossed down the third shot. It joined the other two. I had just drunk more whiskey in ten minutes than I had consumed in my entire life.

I slept well. When I awoke at daylight, the flu was gone. Lord Calvert had been busy while I slept. All those flu germs were too snockered to cause any more trouble. I began to understand how people got started drinking.

ONCE I HAD RECOVERED FROM THE flu and felt healthy again, I returned to work. Selling insurance is a little like a juggler trying to keep three balls in the air. The first ball is prospects. Prospects are potential buyers. Salesmen must find buyers and qualify them as able to buy the product. The second ball is setting appointments to make sales presentations. The third ball is closing the sale, completing the application, and collecting the money.

Salespeople must always be looking for prospects because you don't make any sales when you run out of buyers. I learned a new way of prospecting at a seminar I attended. The Sunday newspaper business section publishes photos and write-ups of people who have gotten promotions at work or have performed outstanding public service. I would scan this section of the paper and select ten of the most promising people. Then I would clip out their picture and put it in an envelope with a crisp one-dollar bill and a short note:

This is a tax-free dollar. I sell them for about four cents each. They come in bundles of a hundred thousand. How many bundles do you want or need? I will call you this coming week so we can schedule an appointment.

Sincerely yours, Bob Finertie.

This method worked well for me and helped me secure interviews with some well-qualified prospects. The most notable was a man who owned a lot of real estate in downtown Buffalo.

THE GM IN BUFFALO WANTED ME TO finish out the first quarter of 1973. However, by the end of January, I had had enough of winter in Buffalo, enough of overcoats, galoshes, ice-scrapers, and separation from my kids. One morning late in January, eleven inches of snow fell during the night. As I swept the snow off my car and started the engine to clear the windshield, a neighbor walked by all bundled up in a wool hat and scarf against the wind and snow. He carried a pipe in his mouth like a snowman. When he passed, he removed his smoke and said, "If you had a horse, you wouldn't have to do that." That snow-storm was the clincher. I turned in my resignation, rented a U-Haul trailer, and aimed it south toward San Antonio. I stayed with friends along the way. Bob and Joyce Harding in New Jersey were childhood friends. Bob and Sue Ramger lived in East Tennessee; Bob and I had run on the track team at Maryville College. My goal had been to reach San Antonio by February fourth to celebrate my daughter Meredith's fifth birthday. Rats, too many miles, not enough hours. When I arrived in River City at two in the morning, everyone was asleep. I was exhausted from all those hours behind the wheel and disappointed that my best efforts had failed to get me there on time. My hyperactive inner critic had a field day berating me for being such an imperfect dad. I am getting better at tuning out some of that criticism, but back then, I had ears like a jackrabbit and a shortage of self-esteem.

Chapter 8

Starting Over

C athy had arranged for me to stay with neighbors across the street until I could find an apartment in San Antonio. After a few days, I moved into the Trade Winds Apartment and called that home during my first year in San Antonio. I was starting over again in a new city. My challenge was to find people to listen to my sales presentation, show them our products, and make some sales. Eddie suggested I call on local businesses offering a service: to help them request a Social Security Statement of earnings. After the printout arrived at my office, I would set an appointment to go over the potential client's retirement benefits with them. Social Security benefits provide the base of a family's retirement income. Payments from their company pension plan, 401 (k), or individual retirement account plus earnings on investments and rental revenue round out the balance. This approach resonated with me, quieting the inner critic who kept nagging me that I was only out to get something with the knowledge that I was also giving something by providing this service.

I would often stop at shopping centers in a prosperous part of town in my search for prospects. I saved time and gas by visiting several businesses at one location. Everybody I talked to would be a qualified prospect as the owner of the company. One day I stopped at a strip mall in Alamo Heights, a wealthy suburb of San Antonio, and made a call on Alamo Diaper Service. Their advertising touted the advantages of cloth diapers over paper throwaways. Cloth diapers fit better, cut back on diaper rash, and eliminated stinky diapers in the garbage.

A bell rang as I entered the store, and a petite blonde with a smile that lit up the room greeted me. "I'm Dana."

"My name is Bob Finertie. I stopped by this morning to offer a service. To help you check on your Social Security account. You can make sure the contributions you send are going into your account, not somebody else's. I can help you request a statement of earnings that will show what is there. I could tell by the way her head was cocked that I had her interest, but there was a hint of skepticism in her expression, as though she were weighing the risk-benefit ratio.

"Here's how it works. We send this card to the Social Security Administration. They will send a printout of your earnings and contributions. Once I have that in hand, I will call to set a time to look it over. Can we take a moment and do that now?"

"Sure" she said, reaching for the card. She placed it on the glass counter, asked if she could use my pen, and started filling in the information.

During this process, I learned that she was vice president of the company and responsible for placing their monthly magazine in OB-GYN doctor's offices. This was how people learned about the advantages of cloth diapers.

We hit it off well from the start. I felt an attraction to her, and I sensed it was mutual. Her openness surprised me. Many people I had approached exhibited more caution. They remained cool or aloof. I could sense they were wondering if this was a scam. I felt flattered when she wanted to continue. By this point, many prospects would have been saying, "I'm not interested." Dana did not say that. I doubt that she woke up that morning aching to know more about Social Security. I was vain enough to think that some of her interest was in me. When people want more of you, their posture remains open. When they want you gone, their body shows that by contracting. In that moment we stayed open to each other, and that was pleasant and affirming.

I put the card in my briefcase and was preparing to leave when Dana said, "Today's the day I take the new issues of our magazine to the various doctor's offices. Want to ride along?"

"I'd love to," I replied, surprised by her offer. Dana drove, and I climbed in on the passenger side. We stopped at several doctors' offices, gathered up the old issues of the diaper magazine, and replaced them with the latest one.

On our way to the car, Dana said, "Let's take a break and grab some lunch. Are you hungry?"

"I'm starved. It feels like a long time since breakfast," I replied.

I found myself curious to see how the rest of this adventure would unfold. I was out of my comfort zone. Most days, I would keep plugging away visiting various businesses until I got ten of the requests for Social Security Statement cards filled out, and then I would return to the office. That practice was equal parts work ethic and OCD. I began to practice staying in the moment, something I had learned at a workshop as an antidote to ruminating in the past or worrying about the future.

"We can do the rest of these later," she said, nodding toward the magazines. "There's a good Mexican restaurant just around the corner. You like Mexican?"

" I grew up in New Jersey. There's not much Mexican food there, but I'm learning to like it."

We made small talk over nachos, salsa, and guacamole while waiting for the entrées to come. Dana said the special of the day looked good, carne asada, huevos ranchero, and refried beans, so we ordered that. When I saw the size of the platters the server set down before us, I knew it was too much food. We could have shared a plate and still had leftovers. This triggers two Great Depression era sayings: "Take all you want but eat all you take" and "Waste not, want not." This amount of food would produce an automatic double infraction.

I made mental notes as we enjoyed the food. Dana was well-groomed and dressed in business casual, an attractive blonde with a sassy haircut. We were at ease together. I felt her warmth and personal interest as we talked. Neither one of us was in a rush to get back to work, but we had work to do, so we delivered the remaining magazines and headed back to her office.

"While you've been driving, I've been thinking, Dana."

"I noticed the gears going around."

"Here's an idea that popped into my mind."

"Shoot."

"New York Life offers a frilly, satin-covered baby book free to people who request one. There's a place inside to record your baby's first words or the date when your baby began to walk. All the pregnant moms need to do is send in a business reply card to get one. What if we put a copy of the baby book in the waiting rooms next to the magazines? Women who come in to see the doctor could scan the baby book while they waited. If they liked it, they could mail in a business reply card. When the card came to me at the office, I could call and arrange a time to take the gift to them. What a great way to meet new prospects. What do you think?"

"I like it. May I see one of the baby books?"

"I don't have one with me, but my office is nearby. If you have time, we can swing by and pick one up now."

"Let's do it."

Dana adored the baby book and agreed to the plan.

On my way back to the office, I pondered the events of the day. Who could have guessed how the day would unfold? I showed up, trying to find new prospects by offering a service. On other days I had encountered a lack of interest or rejection. Today I met Dana. She was welcoming and open to the service. We developed an idea that could become mutually advantageous. We became business friends.

OVER THE NEXT TWO WEEKENDS, I WAS busy out in my garage making display copies for the doctors' offices. I bought a four-by-eight-foot sheet of best grade whiteboard at the lumberyard to match the satin cover on the book. I marked a grid of eight columns on the long side and six on the short side. After making my cuts with a table saw, I had forty-eight pieces of white board that measured eight by twelve inches. I smoothed the rough edges with sandpaper and fastened the books to the whiteboard. I wanted the sample to pique curiosity from the coffee table, where I was hoping they'd be a permanent fixture. And I made the display copies large enough not to slip too conveniently into a woman's purse so that they'd stay put.

I pasted a manilla pocket inside the cover and filled it with business reply cards addressed to me at the office. When the next edition of the diaper magazine came out, I rode around with Dana during her deliveries. This time, as she put down her magazines, I placed a baby book on the table next to them.

The response to this offer was overwhelming. Only one physician asked us to come and remove the display. Within two weeks, my mailbox at work was crammed with reply cards requesting the gift. The general office had to scramble to keep a supply. I called the people who requested the book to arrange a time to deliver it. If they wanted only the book, I mailed it to them. The rest I took in person. I asked them about the baby they were expecting, and I listened. Some wanted a daughter, others preferred a son, but mostly what they all wanted was a healthy baby.

One of the agents in our office had a child born with a hole in her heart. The parents suffered a series of heartaches; their child had five cardiac surgeries during the first four years of life. These disabilities often caused the child to be uninsurable. Insurance companies call them preexisting conditions, which exclude them from getting insurance. Sometimes an insurer will charge a higher premium to offset the greater risk. New York Life offered a policy that guaranteed that a child with a disability can purchase insurance at standard rates. The only stipulation is that the baby is healthy enough to go home from the hospital. As soon as that happens, the policy takes effect. Parents-to-be loved this idea. The business I wrote from this free baby book offer made me one of the leading producers in our office that year. My general manager appointed me supervisor of training in the fall of 1974. I believe this all came together too seamlessly to have been an accident, evidence of the hand of God at work.

Chapter 9

Arnie

....

Desperation stalked me every day. Most days, I managed to keep it at arm's length. I started each morning with a prayer: "God, please grant me enough light to see my next step and enough strength to take it." And God did. My prayer did not make the trail less steep, but it did allow me to keep climbing.

Shortly after I moved into the Antonian Apartments, I hit a dry spell. I tried every arrow in my quiver of sales ideas, and nothing worked. I began to feel incredibly discouraged. Some people seemed leery about the Social Security service. Others didn't want to look at our college savings plan. Even the sure-fire "tax-free dollar" plan failed. In fact, every approach I made drew rejection: "No, not today." "I'm not interested."

One morning, I looked at myself in the men's room mirror while washing my hands and realized that most of what was wrong was me. I felt lethargic and depressed.

I was sure my sadness showed in my demeanor. By three o'clock, I was in no mood to sell anything to anyone, so I decided to call it a day and drove home to my apartment. Maybe a time of swimming and lying in the sun would lift my mood and revive my spirit.

I must have dozed off for a few minutes because I awoke with a start to the sound of a lounge chair scraping along the cement deck. There was another sound I could not place. As I opened my eyes, I saw my neighbor Arnie. Polio had withered his legs, so he walked with crutches that wrapped around his forearms. His irregular gait was producing the noises I couldn't identify. He appeared to be in his thirties, with a full head of auburn hair and a beard. Earlier I had seen him making his way across the parking lot to his car.

"Howdy, neighbor," I said.

"Hi."

"I've seen you a few times coming and going. My name is Bob."

"I'm Arnie."

"We are lucky ducks to be able to soak in this sunshine."

"I hear you, Bob. I had to get out of the office."

"What do you do for a living? Arnie."

"I'm a court recorder."

"What's that?"

"I make a record of the proceedings in the courtroom."

"Oh, I've seen that on TV. You use a machine like a little typewriter."

"I do. It's a steno machine. I type a verbatim copy of what everyone said." Arnie paused for a moment, took a deep breath, puffed out his chest, and said, "I get twenty-five dollars per page."

After allowing that to soak in, Arnie continued, "How about you; what do you do?"

"I work for New York Life."

"The insurance company," he asked.

"That's the one." Usually, this is where the conversation ends. Today it primed the pump."

"I need to talk to you."

"Oh?"

"Yes. I just got a divorce. Part of the settlement requires that I provide health insurance for my wife and children."

"How many kids?

"Three."

"Do you want to do that now or, would you rather set a time for later?"

"Let's do it now. I'll be relieved to have it taken care of."

I felt the adrenaline pumping as I walked to my apartment to pick up my sales literature and rate book. The prospect of writing some business unexpectedly cleared away all the funk I'd been feeling earlier and provided a fresh infusion of energy. I felt like a new man as I sat down at the table on Arnie's patio. Arnie bought four policies that day, one on each of his children and one on his ex-wife. Those sales met my quota for the week and lifted me out of my depression. I raised my eyes toward heaven and thanked God as I walked back to my apartment. I couldn't help wondering about the timing; it was flawless, everything falling into place. I had felt so discouraged earlier that day, and now some power greater than myself had worked it all out for my good.

Chapter 10

Metastasis

....

I awoke on December 20, 1976, to the sound of someone opening the drapes. The light showed a shape at
the window. Was I dreaming?

"Good morning, Robert," the shape said as my eyes
adjusted to the glare. "My name is Susan; I will be your
nurse today."

I felt cheered by the lilt of optimism in her voice, and
now with my eyes in focus, I could see the speaker, young,
attractive, redheaded, and as crisp as her nurse's uniform.
I was thinking, *This is too good to be true. I must have died,
and this is heaven.* Instead, I was in a hospital bed at the
M.D. Anderson Cancer Treatment Center in Houston,
Texas, recovering from surgery that removed the lymph
nodes from my right groin. The procedure is called a
lymphadenectomy. I had an eight-inch incision at the
site (where my leg joins my body) and tubes to allow the
wound to drain into a plastic bag. The surgical team had

decided to remove the lymph nodes and not my leg. Tears welled up behind my eyelids, and my shoulders shook when I saw my leg was still there. My hands trembled as I reached down to confirm it. Thank God. I closed my eyes. As relief sank in, I breathed out a huge sigh.

Susan respected my need for silence and stood by as I processed my feelings.

"Hi, Susan," I finally said. "I'm Bob."

Outside, the clouds blocked out the sun; Susan would be my sunshine for the day. Her beauty and cheerfulness roused me out of drug-induced sleep and fanned a spark of hope as I eased into the new day. Encouragement was what I needed because I had been here for the first surgery (perfusion and incision) a little more than a year ago. The incision from that trip had healed. I had rehabbed my knee in the hot tub at the Antonian. I had regained the strength in that leg and the full range of motion in my knee. The happiness I'd felt over that earlier recovery had given way to depression because I knew that this recovery would be more complicated. Plus, this time, I would be facing a challenging year of chemotherapy, a precaution against metastasis.

Three weeks earlier, on Pearl Harbor Day, I felt concerned about a burning sensation in my right groin. I attributed this sensation to the bites of fire ants, so common in Texas. I had stepped on a nest while mowing the back lawn and suffered several painful, itchy stings. Too scared to connect these symptoms to my melanoma, I chose denial over reality. However, after ten days, the burning had not gone away. It had gotten worse, so I scheduled an appointment with Dr. McMurtry in Houston. A biopsy of the swollen lymph nodes revealed the disease had spread. My heart raced when I heard that news. A chill spread through my body. That biopsy put me on the gurney in the hallway.

But now I was here with Susan, thinking about Christmas—just four days away—while she took my vital signs. I was sick of the disinfectant they use in hospitals and nursing homes that never quite succeeds in masking the odors of sickness and death. I was tired of not getting out of bed, eating hospital food, being awakened by the predawn blood draw, and hurting too long before the nurse brought morphine to ease the pain. I wanted to go home for Christmas.

Most doctors agree that sleep is an essential part of recovery, but then they hand you over to the hospital's demonic regimen of sleep deprivation. Aides stop by to check your vitals, IV techs replace the bags of medication that have dripped dry, or a nurse will come to cancel the warning beep of a monitor and must turn on the overhead lamp so she can see what she's doing. Sleep can be elusive after one has been startled awake, and the adrenaline gets flowing. The wee hours of the morning offer fertile ground for haunting questions. How did I end up here? Why did this happen to me? Was God punishing me? Was I going to survive?

As a human being, I had missed the mark many times, and this awareness triggered an inventory of all the things I had done that might provoke God's anger. Add to these transgressions the big one: I had failed to be the "good boy" Mom implored me to be with the last words she ever spoke. By my acting out, I had moved from a compliant child to a defiant one. Now I knew I was no longer on Mom's kissing list, and I was also afraid God would scratch me off His list. I shook my fist in God's face and shouted, "All these years I have tried to please You, and where has it gotten me? So now I am going to catch up on some of the good stuff I have been missing." And I did in spades.

Before long, I found myself as lost as a man can be. I had alienated my family, sabotaged my ministry, destroyed my standing in the community, and ruined my self-respect. I could see that I had turned off the Interstate onto an unpaved side road. When I looked up, it seemed as though the sign said, "This road leads to death." At that moment, melanoma became my mentor. Its message was, "If you don't change the way you are living, you are going to die." I was ready to listen.

STRANGE HOW CERTAIN LIFE EVENTS become watersheds. One bad lab test or a trip to the operating room becomes a turning point. Afterward, life is not the same. The crisis prompts an internal dialogue about life and death. I think there are more theological discussions in intensive care units than at the seminary. What is essential, and what is not? Will I wake up from this surgery? Anesthesiologists joke about it: "We don't charge much to put you under," they say. "The big bucks are to wake you up." Is this the beginning of the end? Is this the first step of my final journey? Here I am at forty-three, bargaining with God about extending my life, begging Him to add to the number of my days, making bold promises about serving Him that I don't know if I can honor, if only He will allow me to remain in the land of the living.

THAT MORNING, I TOLD SUSAN, "I want to get out of this hospital. I want to be home for Christmas."

"Before we can discharge you, you will need to be able to do three things: One, get in and out of bed by yourself. Two, walk the length of the corridor on crutches. And three, get up from the floor without any assistance—in case you fall." Steps one and two proved easy. Step three seemed impossible because I hurt so much when I tried to move. I made a sales pitch that being home for the holidays with my family and friends would surely be more curative than spending Christmas in the hospital. I was surprised when she agreed.

I left the hospital on December 24th at noon. Two of my coworkers, Eric Rockstroh and Trent Ready, picked me up at the hospital. I couldn't bend my right leg because of the cast, so Eric had brought his father's station wagon. I could ride in the back with my legs fully extended during the three-and-a-half-hour ride to San Antonio. His dad was a funeral director, and I had to chuckle at the irony of riding in the vehicle they used to transport corpses from the hospital to the mortuary and dubbed "the meat wagon."

Eric specialized in breeding Himalayan cats, seal points, and browns. We kidded him about running a "cathouse." He reminded us, "It's a cattery." His broad, open face and rosy cheeks matched his gregarious, extroverted personality. He sported a mustache and Van Dyke goatee that men grew when their hair started thinning on top. The mustache almost succeeded in hiding the childhood scar from harelip surgery. I appreciated his love and compassion as well as his offer to give me a ride home from Houston.

Trent, riding shotgun, was eight years younger. His father, Forrest, was one of my coworkers and a friend. His rugged, handsome face, tan from playing golf, and his relaxed, disarming smile made him a natural chick magnet. Trent had recently graduated from North Texas State University and come on board as an intern at New York Life. He wanted to explore the insurance business as a career opportunity. Trent was on a budget as an intern, so he avoided high-priced lunches. It was more affordable to eat at his place a couple of times a week. He'd slit a hot dog lengthwise, put it in a bun, add American cheese, and nuke it in the microwave just long enough to melt the cheese. It was yummy and slid down smoothly with a Coke and chips.

"You don't know how glad I am to see you guys," I gushed when they came to get me. "People who ride back here usually don't talk much."

Eric laughed and said, "You got that right."

Trent replied, "We're happy to be able to do it."

"Want to go home, Bob?" Eric asked, looking in the rearview mirror.

"I've been yearning for home, but first, I want to go to Claire Carolin's house. She's a therapist in training. I attended a support group she led to help sort myself out. She's having her annual Christmas Eve party, and I don't want to miss it."

I must have dozed off after that. I was in the twilight zone just before waking up when I had an epiphany. I could see that my lifestyle had put a lot of stress on my body, and it was breaking down. Inside, a growing awareness reminded me if I didn't change my lifestyle, I would die. I had tasted the road that led to life, tired of it, and succumbed to the temptation to see what I had been missing. It was then I realized I had turned onto an unmarked side road and knew that if I didn't make a U-turn, I was going to die.

WE STOPPED HALFWAY HOME FOR A BIO break, a stretch, and a snack, so it was quarter to five when Eric pulled into Claire Carolin's driveway. Claire lived with her husband, Jack, and four children in Shavano Park, a gated community west of San Antonio. Their five-bedroom five-bathroom home sat on a two-acre treed lot with an outdoor pool. I had known Claire and Jack, a sculptor, since I relocated from Buffalo to San Antonio a few years earlier. Claire's open arms, cheerful smile, and nurturing presence welcomed us at the door and invited us in. She was approaching her seventh decade yet was full of life and spry beyond her years as she worked to complete her marriage and family therapist training. I had been a regular at her Transactional Analysis and Awareness group on Wednesday evenings. Claire was an essential bead on a necklace of grace-filled people who intersected my life for good. In her TA group, she showed us the difference between a nurturing parent and a critical parent. This distinction was crucial for me. When my mom was alive, she nurtured me, bathed and dressed me, and fixed my meals. She read to me as I was falling to sleep. After she died, most of my nurturing died too. Dad's nurturing came from a critical, judgmental parent with a frown on his face and a belt in his hand. He became even more punishing when he was drinking.

His nurturance turned to neglect as he became more dependent on alcohol, so I wandered around, a starved child looking for a mother surrogate. Claire abounded in love and took me under her wing.

I spent January of 1976 soaking in baths for half an hour three times a day, healing from the surgery. The warm water provided comfort and stimulated circulation around the wound. The doctor recommended adding Epsom salts to promote healing. Bandaging the wound proved tricky due to its location. An idea flashed into my mind: I wondered if a feminine hygiene pad would work. My wife had a supply in the cupboard under the bathroom sink. I checked one for size, perfect. It was absorbent, and adhesive under the peel-away strips would hold it in place. I wondered if I were the first man to wear one.

Chapter 11

Alternative Treatment

··

M y body recoiled at the thought of the twelve
months of chemotherapy that loomed on the
horizon. Friends sent me articles about alternative
forms of treatment. Ellen Smith, a friend, and nurturing
parent from Wyoming, mailed a newspaper clipping that
described unexpected "cures" people were having with
laetrile, the juice squeezed from apricot pits that boasted
all the benefits of chemotherapy without the debilitating
side effects. My heart skipped a beat at the prospect of a
treatment that would leapfrog the nausea, poor appetite,
and hair loss so common with traditional chemotherapy.

I read everything I could find about laetrile and
located a doctor who would administer the treatment.
He worked out of the hospital in Marksville, Louisiana.
I called my health insurance provider to confirm which
charges my policy would cover and was surprised to
learn that they would pay both the hospital costs and the
physician's fees. When I decided to go for it, the doctors

at M.D. Anderson Hospital said, "You're wasting your time and money." I heard what they were saying, but the idea still appealed to me. Ellen thought the medical community had their treatment ass-backward, attacking cancer with chemicals that destroyed the healthy cells along with the diseased ones. She favored an approach that built up a patient's immune system to empower the body to overcome the disease. So did I. Plus, deep inside, I was tired of being cut and diced and probed. This alternative treatment offered a time-out where I could rest and recuperate before the next round of assaults on my body.

I called the doctor in Marksville who arranged admission for February 15, 1976. The protocol extended over ten days. Although my insurance covered the hospital and the physician's charges, it did not pay for the medication, as laetrile was not FDA-approved to treat melanoma. I called my boss, Eddie, in San Antonio to see if I could borrow $2800 to pay for the drug.

"Of course," he said. "We want you to get better." Eddie had a big heart and was always generous.

While driving from San Antonio to Marksville in mid-February, I had second thoughts about following a nontraditional treatment plan. I had always had a "good boy" persona. I was one to do as the doctors recommended. My mother's voice still echoed inside my head though she had died when I was eight and a half. She "tsk-tsked" my rebellious choice and noncompliant actions as I transferred my things from the suitcase to the dresser and closet, and the nursing staff helped me get comfortable in my hospital digs.

The place looked like a regular hospital, with

admissions, nursing stations, and rooms, but I wondered, *What kind of hospital would administer an unapproved treatment protocol? The Twilight Zone* theme song rang in my ears in a closed-circuit loop. The entire operation felt clandestine.

At supper, I learned the doctor had prescribed a diet to help me shed a few pounds. I enjoyed the shrimp and rice but missed the cocktail sauce, and the salad needed dressing. Even so, a full stomach helped me to relax. Tired from the long drive, I dozed off and slept through the night.

The following day after breakfast, the doctor explained what would happen. "The nurses will administer your treatment intravenously, twice a day for seven days, and we'll keep you on a low-fat diet. Any questions?"

"Only one. May I have coffee with breakfast?"

"One cup, black. See you tomorrow."

I lay in a hospital bed, relieved to be in a private room, not having to interact with anybody. The nurse entered the room with a "Good morning, Robert," pushing a cart with an IV setup.

"Good morning, and you can call me 'Bob.'"

"Bob it is. I'm Kelly. I'm here to start an IV to administer your medication," she said, pointing to a plastic bag on the cart.

In it was the laetrile, juice extracted from apricot pits, that was going to spare me the debilitating side effects of traditional chemotherapy.

"I appreciate your skill in finding the vein. Not everybody can do that."

"Thank you, I've had a lot of practice. You can relax now, Bob, while the IV drips. I'll check back in a few minutes. Here's the call button if you need me."

"Okeydokey."

The juice dripped, and I dozed off, pain-free and without nausea. The next thing I knew, they were waking me for lunch. I had more trouble with the diet than with my treatment. At discharge, I obtained a month's supply of the "juice" to take back to Texas. I thanked the doctor and the nursing staff for their TLC. I loved the feeling of strength returning to my body. Ten days of a special diet plus the infusions of laetrile combined to produce a state of hopeful optimism as I climbed behind the wheel and set out for home.

BACK IN SAN ANTONIO, I SLAMMED into reality as I looked for a registered nurse to administer the laetrile intravenously. Before I left for Marksville, my sister-in-law, a nurse, had agreed to do it, so I called to let her know I was back from Louisiana with the juice. "I'm looking for a time to do the infusion," I said.

She hesitated. I grew nervous.

"Bob, I know I said I could do that for you, but I looked into it more closely while you were away. My supervisor at work cautioned me against it. I could lose my nurse's license if I do it."

"That really sucks," I said. I couldn't contain my disappointment. "I was counting on you. I paid for the juice and brought it home with me based on our agreement. Now you're saying you can't do the infusion? What am I gonna do?"

"I'm so sorry, Bob," Carolyn said, "but I didn't know what was at stake until I looked into it. I wanted to do that for you, that's my job, but not at the risk of losing my license. I'm sorry."

After hanging up the phone, I seethed inside. I wanted to wring Carolyn's neck. The disappointment was crushing. I felt I was being squeezed in a trash compactor with no way out and no on/off switch.

What hit the hardest was the loss of control. The feeling of autonomy that I had worked so hard to achieve by engineering this period of respite from being "done to" all went up in smoke when Carolyn said no.

I ASKED TWO OTHER NURSE FRIENDS if they could help me out. They felt inclined to as a favor to me but politely declined, unwilling to assume the risk. I'd obtained the expensive drug, but if I had to travel to Louisiana four times a month for the IVs to be administered, the treatment plan became unsustainable. I was stuck with a month's supply of laetrile and no way to get it into my body. A heaviness spread through me at this turn of events, and I let out a huge sigh. I winced as I lifted the lid to the trash can and dropped the juice inside, a total loss.

There was no way to measure how much the laetrile helped me at the cellular level, since there was no control group. I do know the trip to Marksville allowed me some autonomy in managing my treatment. I stepped out of the victim position where medical techs were doing unpleasant things to me and took a break. It also provided a time for healing from the surgical assault on my body and the psychic trauma of learning that I had what could be a terminal illness.

With the laetrile regimen financially unsustainable, I realized that I would be an outlier in a battle to beat cancer without any allies at my side, so I abandoned my

Lone Ranger approach, changed my tack, and opted to enter the standard, FDA-approved chemotherapy protocol for people with melanoma. This choice had science behind it and offered the best chance for recovery.

Chapter 12

Traditional Chemotherapy

N ot being able to use the laetrile dashed my hopes of
finding a less arduous cure for melanoma. I realized
there was no escape from chemo-triggered, anxiety-filled
dreams that interrupted my sleep and upset my usually
predictable body functions. I had heard stories about the
unpleasant side effects of chemotherapy, typically nausea,
vomiting, and diarrhea. I had seen how it ravaged the
body, caused weight loss, and produced the pale, waxy look
of sickness. I saw how many chemo patients wore hats
and scarves to hide their hair loss. I regarded chemo as a
last-ditch effort to improve my chances of survival. The
evidence was clear that it helped some cancer patients live
longer, but many patients didn't make it. Fear and resistance tied knots in my gut because deep down I knew I
might go through all these infusions and lacerations and
still not make it. Nevertheless, I didn't want to wake up
one day regretting that I hadn't given myself every opportunity to survive, so I chose to keep the appointment with
the oncologist, despite my doubts.

On Monday, March 1, 1976, Lynn drove me to the doctor's office in Houston where we listened as the oncologist outlined the procedure. "On the first of each month, you will begin your course of chemotherapy, and it will last for five days. Because the effects are cumulative, you will feel wretched by the end of the week."

As he spoke, my jaw tightened. I could feel resistance building, as when you're going up the starting hill of a roller coaster. A cable pulls you up, and ratchets click behind you so you can't go backward. Time drags and offers a longer interval for the buildup of dread. When you arrive at the top and look down to see where you're going, there's a moment of stark disbelief. *Oh no, tell me that's not where I'm going.* Once, when I was riding The Rattler at Fiesta Texas with my daughter Holly, she wanted to get out at the top. I understood. Then you're on your way. It felt so unfair. I didn't sign up for this. Most people probably didn't want to do it but did it anyway. I needed to learn more.

"On the fifteenth of the month," he continued, "you'll come back for the BCG part of the treatment."

Those three letters stand for Bacillus Calmette and Guerin after the two doctors discovered the serum that caused the dark spot to disappear when injected near a melanoma site.

"You'll come here for the first treatment, and the nurse will demonstrate the procedure so your wife can do that part at home instead of having to drive over here. Any questions?"

Compassion softened his face as he spoke. I felt caring in his voice as he offered the option to eliminate much of the driving.

"Yes," I replied, "I do have a question." I told him how I'd eaten healthy foods, exercised, and taken good care of my body all my life. I didn't drink alcohol or do drugs. "Why should I let you put chemicals in my veins that are so strong the IV nurse wears a protective Plexiglass shield and heavy rubber gloves?" I asked, pointedly.

"That's a fair question," he said, moving in closer and looking me straight in the eye. "Here's what we've found. If we line up one hundred people who have what you have against the wall and don't treat them, at the end of two years, only fifteen will be alive."

In that moment, I saw myself alive and well, seated with my wife, ten years down the road. This vision of hope pierced through my darkness and depression, a gift of grace.

"On the other hand, if we treat them, we can turn those odds around." Here he got personal, scooted his stool closer, and said, "If it were my body, I would do it."

His statement convinced me to go ahead with the treatment despite my doubts. I decided I would endure the side effects to improve my chances to live.

As we left his office and headed to the car park, I said to Lynn, "Well, Honey, we're off on a new adventure."

"We are. It's not one I would have chosen, but when you've got melanoma, this is the right place to be, and chemo is the right thing to do."

"If I said I wasn't scared, I'd be lying." Looking into her eyes, I added, "I'm so glad you're here to walk through this with me."

"I'm not going anywhere," she said, reaching out with comfort and assurance as she took my hand in hers.

In Africa they have a saying that feels right here. When you are totally at peace about something, you say, "my heart sat down." My heart sat down.

I SLEPT FITFULLY DURING THE NIGHT before chemo began. Fear and apprehension chipped away at my peace. As a longtime bodybuilder, I was apprehensive about weight loss and general weakness. On Monday morning, March 8, 1976, Lynn drove me to the IV center for my ten o'clock appointment. The receptionist welcomed us with a cheerful "good morning" and a smile. I felt grateful for that courtesy, but her surface cordiality failed to calm my fears about what was soon to happen. Lynn sensed my trepidation and squeezed my hand. I was glad that she had come with me.

My gut felt as shaky as a bowl of Jell-O at the beginning of this journey into the unknown. Several questions troubled me: How intense would the nausea be? How long would it last? Knowing that the chemo had no ability to discriminate between diseased and healthy cells, I worried about how many "good guys" would have to die along with the "bad guys."

The war inside my body at the cellular level would be intense, and my survival depended on the outcome. My mind became a second battlefield. How would I maintain positive thoughts and keep my mind focused as I faced troubling questions? What if this didn't work? Once cancer has spread to other parts of your body, it's a challenge to avoid the haunting question: Where's it going to show up next?

The physical arrangement of the IV center did little

to relieve my anxiety. Think barracks with twenty bunks on each side of the room, but instead of beds, there were chairs: stainless steel chairs upholstered with blue-gray Naugahyde, and an IV tree attached to the arm. The IV poles reminded me of masts on the sailboats at the San Francisco Yacht Club. Gray-and-white walls and gray linoleum floors felt cold and practical without a hint of comfort or warmth. I longed for some art on the walls and carpet on the floors. As the nurse led me to my designated chair, I felt like I was entering prison with an indeterminate sentence.

She started an IV of saline to make sure of a good connection before hooking up the payload. I cringed when she approached with her Plexiglas face shield and heavy-duty rubber gloves, rolling an IV setup and three bags of chemical treatment on a steel cart.

"We'll do these one at a time using a slow drip," she said. "It will take about an hour and a half in all. The hardest part will be having to sit here that long. I hope you brought something to read."

"I did. My wife has it in her purse. Thank you." Even though I was shaking with fear, at least I could be polite.

I had survived the first surgery—perfusion and incision—in 1975 and lived through the removal of the lymph nodes in my right groin—lymphadenectomy—in 1976. Now, I was facing a year of chemical assault that promised to be unpleasant at best and could not guarantee a cure. Chemotherapy was the best hope doctors had to offer and my last-ditch effort to survive. I whispered to myself, "Take my hand, Lord. I'm on a scary journey, and it may be a one-way trip."

I STARTED TREATMENTS AT MD Anderson in Houston, but in the second month I was able to transfer my treatments to the San Antonio Cancer Therapy & Research Center and avoid all that travel. The first six months' treatment went by quickly and were not pleasant but were not unbearable. Before the seventh session, I noticed I was drooling, and my body was full of pre-infusion anxiety. I felt a great aversion to going to the clinic. The doctor prescribed Thorazine, an antianxiety medication, to get through it. Just before they started the IV, I'd lower my pants for a shot in the butt. I felt like a zombie drooling and numb, unsteady on my feet with a shuffling gait.

You may wonder about the effects of the chemical assault on my body. I went for the treatment at ten in the morning and came home around noon, spending the rest of the day hugging the toilet. In addition, the smell of Lynn cooking meals left me nauseous and without appetite until about eight that night, when I could stomach bland fare. Thankfully, I slept through the evening until I returned to chemo the next morning. This continued for five days in a row followed by three weeks off, month after month.

On the fifteenth of each month, Lynn and I proceeded with the BCG therapy at home. This consisted of marking my body with a grid, using a needle with a sharp edge to break the skin. Each month we would choose a different site—my upper arm, my thigh—alternating sides. The abrasion, six rows on each side, like a crossword puzzle on the skin, enabled the medicine to penetrate. Once the grid was complete, the paste was applied with a tongue depressor and worked into the needle pricks. Lynn grimaced as she cut my skin, sometimes deeper than needed due to the couple of beers she had beforehand to steel herself. But somehow, we got through it, and Lynn would use her hair dryer to dry the area before bandaging me. Lynn hated doing it, which I could appreciate because I'd also hate to have to do that to someone I love.

I ENDURED THE YEAR OF TRADITIONAL chemo in 1977 like a fighter in a twelve-round heavyweight bout. Every month when it was time for chemo, my stomach churned. Like a fighter, I heard the bell and asked myself, *Do I want to keep on doing this?* I forced myself back into the ring for all twelve rounds.

In a checkup after the treatment ended, the doctor said, "There's no evidence of cancer in your body." To prove it, he showed me a body-length CT scan in the lightbox. Joy flooded my body, and afterward, Lynn and I skipped together to the parking lot. We bought a new house and enjoyed life out of the shadow of melanoma for the next few years.

One might ask, *What is the proper response to being spared by grace?* One thing I did was go to the DMV and get a personalized license plate with B1SELF on it. I had learned not to be a people-pleaser but to do what I wanted with my life instead. I wanted to do some of the things God intended me to do with my life. I started a thanksgiving journal in which I listed every day some of the things I was personally grateful for. I didn't want to forget all the blessings God had bestowed on me, chief among them the freedom from melanoma.

Sadly, the years of sickness and treatment, plus Lynn's new and growing dependence on alcohol, took a toll on our marriage. We divorced in 1980.

Chapter 13

New Growth

....

As I continued my healing journey, I joined Adult Children of Alcoholics, an offshoot of Al-Anon. Finally, I had found my tribe and began some much needed emotional healing. There I made some wonderful friends, including Leslie. We got to know each other outside of meetings as the group went to dinner or played volleyball. Our relationship grew, and we started playing tennis and visiting museums together. I loved attending her Texas Bach Choir concerts and the way her face filled with joy whenever she sang.

Changes were happening at New York Life, and I went from being the hero to the goat in the eyes of my new manager, who replaced Eddie after his retirement. I told him I would resign at the end of a year if he no longer wanted me. He took me up on my offer right after my birthday. It was once again time to start over.

I interviewed locally and with Presbyterian Ministers Fund in Philadelphia. Coincidentally, the CEO of
Presbyterian Ministers Fund was Bob Lamont, under
whom I had felt the call to ministry. He didn't know
this until I shared it with him then. It helped solidify my
relationship with him, and I knew the job was mine if I
wanted it. But they required me to move to an airport
hub because I would need to travel extensively. Thinking
it over, I decided against the job.

Instead, I went to an interview at Businessmen's
Insurance in Kansas City, Missouri. While I was there,
I was scheduled for a day with five or six top managers
of the company. When the morning arrived, it had
snowed more than eight inches overnight, and none of
the managers could get to the office. I was staying at a
nearby hotel so could walk there. The executive secretary
didn't know what to do with me and asked if there was
anything else I wanted to do while I was in Kansas City.
I said yes, I had long wanted to go to Lee's Summit,
Missouri, the headquarters of Unity Church. I wanted
to see if it was "the real thing." I also wanted to meet
their poet laureate, James Dillet Freeman, because I'd been
reading his poetry since 1975 when I subscribed to their
devotional, *The Daily Word.*

She requisitioned a driver and car to take me to Lee's
Summit and waited for me to visit. It just so happened it
was lunch time when I arrived, so I went to the cafeteria
to have a bite. I saw a man with long white hair who
had to be Jim Freeman He had penned a poem called
"I Am There" which James Irwin, one of the astronauts
on Apollo 15, left in microfiche at the Hadley-Apennine
region of the moon. Previously Astronaut Buzz Aldrin

had carried Freeman's beloved "Prayer for Protection" poem with him on the Apollo 11 moon landing:

Prayer for Protection by James Dillet Freeman
The light of God surrounds me;
The love of God enfolds me;
The power of God protects me;
The presence of God watches over me.
Wherever I am, God is!

I took my lunch over to his table and introduced myself. "You must be James Freeman. I've been reading your poetry since 1975 and wanted to meet the man who penned it." He left his colleagues and asked me to join him at a nearby table where we could talk. This chance relationship blossomed into one of the most precious of my life.

The next day the roads cleared, and I interviewed for and was offered the job, which I readily accepted. It meant leaving Leslie and San Antonio, but the position was a good fit for me. The guys thought Leslie would surely move to Kansas City to join me and were delighted to learn she was coming for a visit. Over the course of two months, we saw each other every other week and talked on the phone daily. But living apart was so painful to us that we agreed that I would move back to San Antonio, and we would get married.

I married Leslie on June 10, 1988. We decided we would defer having a family until I finished a masters in marriage and family therapy at St. Mary's College in San Antonio. I knew from experience it would be tough getting through school if we had little ones to care for. I graduated in 1990 and then began an internship, followed by establishing a private practice. I had clients from two separate internships at St. Mary's College and Jewish Family Services. Both supervisors asked me to continue with them because of the strong, trusting relationships that I had forged with them. They became my first private practice clients.

Now that my new career was established, we could focus on starting a family, and we had twin girls in September of 1992.

Chapter 14

More Medical Issues

....

In March of 1993, the doctor diagnosed the pain in my abdomen as gallstones and removed my gallbladder. Following surgery, the symptoms worsened and prompted more tests. In May, a total obstruction of my bowel provoked a trip to the emergency room. When my vomit turned brown, a sign blinked on and off in my head: *This is serious.* A battery of tests revealed a growth obstructing the bowel. Dr. Bratcher removed a grapefruit-sized tumor and fourteen inches of my colon. The procedure is called a sigmoid resection. This incident was thankfully unrelated to the earlier melanoma, a fear that doctors expressed to Leslie prior to surgery.

I lay in bed at Methodist Hospital, drifting in and out of consciousness from the drugs they were giving me to control the pain, when I was startled by the sound of the elevator doors opening across the hall. I looked up to see Leslie, wearing a big smile and pushing a double-wide stroller containing our fraternal twins, Holly and Heather. She parked them as close as she could to the bed so I could see them and said, "I want to be sure you know what you're living for." Her heart-to-heart message brought tears of joy. She followed it up with a hug, a kiss, and an "I love you."

In that moment, I knew how lucky I was to be alive, to be married to Leslie, and to be Holly and Heather's father. It was after this surgery when the chemo wasn't working that I wanted to visit Ellen Smith in Wyoming.

MY ABDOMEN HURT WHEN I MOVED, reminding me that I was healing from surgery. Dr. Bratcher had removed a cancerous tumor and part of my colon. He then skillfully rejoined the colon and checked for leaks. Finding none, he closed me up and sent me home.

During a post-op checkup, Dr. Bratcher peeled off the gauze bandages covering the staples that held the wound closed. I flinched reflexively when the tape stuck to the skin near the incision. The row of sixteen stainless steel staples looked like the laces on a football. The thought of uncrimping those staples sent a shudder through my body. The skin had grown over and around them, so it didn't look easy. A neon sign "*PAINFUL!*" blinked a warning in my mind. Sensing my uneasiness, the doctor said, "I know it looks painful getting those staples out, but this little gadget saves the day." He picked up a pair of pliers from the sterilized tray.

"I'll show you how they work."

He inserted one tip under the staple, and as he squeezed the handles together, the pressure bent the middle of the fastener down and forced the ends up so he could remove it with tweezers. I scarcely felt it except for a few where my skin had grown over them. Now I had healed enough to begin chemotherapy. My belly softened as he explained that the chemo was five days in a row the first week, followed by one day a week for a year. That seemed easy to me after the earlier twelve-month ordeal I referred to as my "Bataan death march."

Each day I went to the IV center at ten in the morning and received the infusion. I thought I'd try something different this time while I was going through chemo. So I left the IV center with a roll of quarters. For ten dollars, I could have an afternoon of fun at the arcade. They had a pinball machine I liked with flippers and a spot where you could flip it in if you timed it right for a special bonus! I worked that flipper hard and became proficient in picking up the bonus. Over time, I got to the top ten scores and got free games as a result. As a special bonus, I got coupons for high scores that could be redeemed for gifts at the bar. The machine played for a quarter, but by inserting four quarters at a time, I'd receive five plays. On the week of chemo, I was there at the machine putting in four quarters to get my free game, winning additional free games now and then with a high score, and collecting all those coupons. Kids would stop by and notice because I regularly won a long ribbon of coupons. They spit out of the machine and ran over the floor. I kept them in a shoe box, and at the end of the year, I traded them in for an electronic thesaurus.

The absence of nausea meant I didn't have to hug the toilet this round, but the effects were cumulative. By the end of the week, my mouth was so sore I couldn't eat. I felt a growing weakness from the effects of the chemical assault, now made worse by the lack of food. Leslie prepared applesauce and scrambled eggs for supper, something that would go down easily. I wanted that food so badly, but I hurt too much to swallow it. She called Dr. Crook for advice. He said, "What you need is some "Heavenly Pink." That's what my patients call it. It's Pepto Bismol and lidocaine, and it will help you get some food down."

He was right, and I let out a huge sigh of relief.

As the second part of my treatment, the doctor prescribed worming pills, the kind ranchers give their goats to prevent them from having worms.

"I know it sounds strange," he said, "but we've found that animals who are on this medication never develop colon cancer."

During my most recent visit to Dr. Crook, my oncologist drew me aside and said, "Bob, can we talk about something serious?" I held my breath. My stomach knotted as the importance of his question sank in. My thoughts raced. *Oh my God, I may have run out of luck. Could this be the beginning of the end?* I could taste fear.

"The results of your CEA test are not where we'd like to see them," he told me. CEA is medical shorthand for carcinogenic embryonic antigen. It's a way to measure how your body is doing in its fight against cancer. "The low side of the range is two point five," he said. "Your latest test result is five point eight." An uncomfortable pause followed the shock of that disclosure. As the meaning set in, my pulse quickened, and my palms got sweaty. This latest news staggered me.

Every cell in my body was crying out for my healing place. I wanted some emotional support from Ellen, the kind that I had gotten from Mack and Ellen when I faced cancer the first time, almost seventeen years ago. Leslie agreed to drive to the Smiths' ranch in Wyoming, which I affectionately called Smith Patch, my healing place.

Mack and Ellen were not members of my biological family, but they were members of my heart family that I chose because of their nurturing and accepting ways. I craved their love. I longed for the big sky, the stars at night, and the Milky Way. I wanted to feast my eyes on the amber waves of grain. As we drove onto their ranch, a host of pickup trucks and the horse and cattle trailers announced that it was branding day. This exciting event drew a crowd at Smith Patch on the middle Wednesday of June every year.

Ellen came out on the back steps to greet us. The dust behind our car tipped her off to our arrival. A motley pack of dogs surrounded us as we approached her. My belly trembled with emotion when we embraced. "Well, hi," she said. "I've been eager to meet these twins."

"This is Holly, she's the firstborn, and this is Heather, who was born an hour and fifteen minutes later. This is Ulrika, our au pair, who helps take care of the twins."

"Oh my, they're adorable. Come on inside. I'll introduce you to some of the cooks and show you where you'll sleep. Excuse the mess; my house is clean enough to be healthy and dirty enough to be comfortable."

LESLIE HAD VISITED SMITH PATCH BACK in 1987, a few months after Mack died but before we were married. I had already arrived to hunt mule deer, a trip I had made annually for the past twenty years. The season ran the first two weeks of October. Ten of us had just finished breakfast and were about to leave for the field when the phone rang. Ellen took it and said, "Bob, it's for you."

It was Leslie calling from Denver. "Hi, honey. Before you left, you said I'd probably like it in Wyoming. I thought about it and told myself, *He's right,* so I got a ticket. My flight arrives in Cheyenne at eleven fifteen. Can you pick me up?"

"Of course. Wow, this is a big surprise. I'm excited."

"Okay, see you in Cheyenne."

Geno, a cousin from Iowa, said, "Boy, she must be special for Bob to miss opening day."

Butterflies took over my stomach at this sudden change of plans. I felt both excited to see Leslie and disappointed to miss hunting on opening day. I knew I would hear about it from the guys when I got back from the airport.

Both of us were hungry, so we had a bite at the airport before heading north to the ranch, an hour-and-a-half drive. As we pulled up to the shop and parked, Doc Jacobi was skinning his deer. He was Geno's friend and a surgeon from Cedar Rapids. We got out of the car and walked over to Doc.

"Nice deer, Doc. You scored early."

"It was the first one we saw."

"I'd like you to meet Leslie. Honey, this is Doc Jacobi."

"Glad to meet you, Doc," she said, averting her eyes from the bloody carcass. Her body suggested she didn't want to be there. When Doc tossed the scraps to the dogs, she put her hand over her mouth and walked toward the house.

"See you later, Doc. We're going up to see Ellen."

Ellen had seen the dust behind my car and was on her way to meet us.

"Hi, Ellen, what a joy to see you."

"Well, hi." She opened her arms wide, and I started to sob as I hugged her.

"You must be Leslie. Welcome. I've been eager to meet you. I knew you had to be special for Bob to miss opening day. Let's go inside where we can visit. I'll show you where you can sleep."

WE FOLLOWED ELLEN UPSTAIRS TO the kitchen. She paused at the top to unlatch the gate that kept the grandchildren from falling down the stairs and secured it behind us. We picked our way across the kitchen floor to avoid the pots and pans the kids had pulled out of the cabinets and the wooden clothespins they were trying to drop into a glass milk bottle.

"It helps with their hand-eye coordination," Ellen said, referring to the clothespin drop.

Leslie wasn't a hunter, so she stayed behind with Ellen. The two of them connected. Ellen showed her the milk separator and explained, "After you milk the cows, and that milk has cooled, you pour the milk into the separator and turn it on. It spins at high speed, separating the cream from the skim milk. Cream comes out this spout and skim milk this one." Then she poured the cream into a churn and handed it to Leslie. "Keep turning this crank, and we'll have butter for supper." She put the skim milk in a pot, placed it on the stove and turned on the gas. Before long, as if by magic, the heat caused curds to form on top. Ellen scooped them off with a strainer and soon had a bowl of cottage cheese. One bucket of cow's milk provided a beverage to drink, cream for your oatmeal, butter for your toast, and cottage cheese to put on your peach halves. Ellen also showed Leslie how to can bread-and-butter pickles and how to make chokecherry jelly.

Royce and I came back to the ranch early on the day I bagged my deer. Royce was Ellen's third son, who ran the ranch after Mack died in March of 1987. He was a mountain of a man yet gentle as a lamb unless provoked. Mack used to drive me around the ranch in a silver Jeep to help me find a deer, and Royce assumed that function after his dad died. I'd ride shotgun and help by opening and closing the gates. This was a working ranch, so the rule of the West prevailed: If the gate's closed when you find it, close it after you, if it's open when you find it, leave it open. Mack pulled my leg a lot. He'd drive up to a gate that was already open and stop for me to open it. Then, as I was climbing out of the Jeep he'd say, "I'll get this one" and grin.

I miss Mack, his welcoming presence, his sense of humor, his infectious grin, and his nurturing ways. He was like a dad to me. I regret that Leslie never got to meet him. One of the things I liked the most about Mack was his view of stewardship. He had worked hard to acquire the land and fence it, digging the post holes by hand, thousands of them. His hands bore testimony to all that labor. One day, as we drove around the place checking the windmills to make sure the cows had water, he said, "I never went into debt to buy land. I only bought what I had the money to pay for." It was clearly his place. He had worked for it, paid for it, and held the deed. Yet he didn't see himself as its owner. In his view, he was the trustee of the property, in charge of helping as many people as possible enjoy the land. If anyone stopped by the ranch and asked to hunt, they were welcome. He reserved a section of the ranch for that purpose. But if you trespassed without permission, you'd be escorted off the property, gently if possible, forcibly if necessary.

As we passed the ranch house, I saw feet kicking high in the air and heard childlike laughter. Leslie had found the swing Mack built for the children. She was swinging with wild abandon as high as she could go. A smile as wide as a Halloween pumpkin graced her face, and her whole body shouted, *Joy!* I grabbed my camera and captured the moment. I call this picture "Joy to the World."

THAT WAS THEN, AND THIS IS NOW. After greeting all the guests, we unloaded the car, put our things in our rooms, and drove out to the corral to observe the action. I had just gotten a new Canon camera with an autofocusing feature, and I was eager to try it out. The branding offered tons of scenes to capture. The roundup, gathering cattle from other pastures so they'd be in one place, *click*. Cowboys whirling their lassos to separate the calves from their mamas, *click*. Strong arms holding the calves while the brand was applied, *click*. Attaching a color-coded tag to the ear to show who owned them, *click*.

Leslie had seen as much as she wanted of branding in about fifteen minutes. She didn't like the sounds and smells, and with two yearlings of her own in tow, she winced at the pain the cowboys inflicted on the calves. "Too much like torture," she said as she gathered up her things and headed back to the ranch house. Ulrika looked on with rapt attention. Coming from Sweden, she'd never seen a roundup, branding, or a cowboy. Now she was having an immersion experience with all three. Leslie released her from childcare duties so she could stay to observe. Most of the cowboys were older hands, but there were a few late teenagers like her. Her cheeks flushed when she saw Walden, a lanky local cowboy who hadn't seen many stunning blondes from Sweden. His goo-goo eyes spoke volumes about what he thought of Ulrika.

I left that to unfold as it would and looked for more photo ops. I felt cheered, soaking in the sights and sounds of the branding, the whir of the lariat, *click*, and the cowboys' guttural commands to their horses as they cut the calves from the herd, *click*. They herded the calves into a pen for branding and released the cows back to the pasture. The noise level surprised me. When five hundred calves bawled for their moms, and five hundred cows bawled for their calves, it generated a lot of decibels. The roar of gas burners heating the branding irons made it even louder. Repulsive smells of burning hair and hide floated through the air in small puffs as the red-hot irons made their distinctive marks on the calves' buttocks. I was going through some challenging stuff myself with chemotherapy and its unpleasant side effects, but at that moment, I was grateful to be a two-legged critter.

We spent a week at the Smiths', savoring Ellen's cooking and eating vegetables she had grown in her garden: cucumber-vinegar salad, corn on the cob, and juicy sliced tomatoes. Nobody could resist her fried bread with hand-churned butter, honey, and elderberry jelly. Along with the food, I soaked in her nurturing and TLC.

Once the crowd cleared from the branding, Royce gassed up the Bronco and drove us around the ranch. We saw a herd of mule deer first, named for their oversized ears. They stood nervously and eyed us from a distance. When they scented us, they grew fearful and bounded away. They don't run or trot; they bound—all four hooves off the ground simultaneously—covering several feet per bound. We saw several groups of antelope, the least social of the prairie residents and the most easily spooked. Often as we came over a hill, we'd spot some pronghorns less than a hundred yards away. They'd take off over the other side of the mound and disappear. The next time we saw them, they'd be a quarter mile distant. If we were lucky, an occasional jackrabbit or a coyote would cross our path. The aromatic smell of sagebrush and greasewood filled the cabin of the Bronco as Royce drove across the prairie.

The weight of the vehicle crushed the bushes as we ran over them and released their aromas. Delightful. I wished I could have put some of that in a bottle.

I would have liked to stay for the rest of the summer, but that was not possible. When our week was over, we said our goodbyes reluctantly, gave hugs all around, and thanked the Smiths for their hospitality.

Chapter 15

Epiphany

....

Tears rolled down my cheeks as I got in the van and headed south toward Texas. Leslie did the driving, Ulrika cared for the children, and I slept. I was still healing from the surgery, and the painkillers made me drowsy. When we rounded a curve or stopped, I opened my eyes and looked around to see where we were, and dozed off again.

When we were about thirty-five miles from home, I woke up. We were almost to Comfort, Texas, where US 87 joins I-10. As I was getting my bearings, I saw something out of the corner of my eye. I looked to see if Leslie saw it, too. She did not. She was paying attention to her driving, focused on the road ahead. It appeared at the top of the windshield behind the rearview mirror. I did a double take to get a closer look. Whatever it was, it started fuzzy, like looking at the Andromeda galaxy with binoculars. As it came more into focus, I could see my mom and dad up there in the clouds, near enough to see them clearly, but not close enough to touch.

I blinked in astonishment. I thought I must be dreaming. When I looked again, they were still there. With loving thoughts emanating from their eyes, they spoke to me. "Bobby, you're going to be okay," they said before they disappeared.

Nothing like that had ever happened to me before, and I longed to extend this reunion. I didn't know whether to believe it or not. I sat quietly in the car for some time, pondering this extraordinary encounter. The message offered the reassurance I needed to hear. I wanted to tell everyone about it, but I didn't know yet if I could trust it. I had been fooled before by mirages while driving; you know, when you see water on the road ahead and would bet money that it was real, but there's no water there. Was my mind playing tricks on me? I wasn't sure whether to share it with Leslie. She might write me off as spaced out on drugs or crazy. I stayed silent for a long time, savoring this magical moment to myself and longing for it to be true.

A SURVEY REPORTED THAT OVER 40 percent of Americans had a transcendental experience at least once in their lives, and 20 percent had several. Respondents said they had never discussed these experiences with anyone. The reason? "They would think I was crazy." (*Yoga and the Quest for the True Self*, Stephen Cope, Bantam Books, 1999, p.39)

Chapter 16

Follow-up Visit

....

A fter the epiphany on US 87, I could scarcely wait
for my next appointment with Dr. Crook. I felt
hopeful and encouraged by my parents' message but still
uncertain I could trust it. My body crackled with excitement and cowered in fear as my follow-up visit drew
near. I both longed and dreaded knowing the results of
my latest CEA tests.

The waiting room at the Oncology Department in
Methodist Hospital bristled with activity underneath a
pall of potentially disturbing news. Forty souls waited
with shallow breathing, wringing their hands as they
awaited lab results that would change their destiny. I
wondered, too, as I listened for my name.

"Robert," the nurse said, and it took a moment to
register because most people call me "Bob." My pulse
quickened as I got up and followed the nurse to the examining room. It felt more like a courtroom, because here

I would receive my sentence. But first, she checked my vitals and asked, "How are you doing?"

"Fine," I said, though other words like *scared, terrified,* or *conflicted* would ring truer.

"Doctor will be with you shortly," she said as she left the room.

I doubted that because I'd spent a lot of time waiting for physicians who get derailed by emergencies as the day wore on. This day was different. Within minutes, Dr. Crook knocked gently on the door and entered the room with a hint of anticipation.

"I know you're wondering," he said, "so I won't keep you waiting."

I nodded.

"Your tests show a significant improvement from five point eight last visit to five point three today."

Relief flooded through my body as I heard this news. Tears filled my eyes and gratitude my heart.

"The chemo is doing its job, and that's encouraging," he said. "One robin does not mean it's spring, but it's a welcome harbinger. We'll continue to follow your progress monthly to track your numbers."

I heard the relief in his voice and felt it in my soul, where profound truths are known.

Deep inside, I wanted to say, "I knew they would be better," after what I'd seen on US 87, but I wasn't ready to go there yet with him. The moment for a reveal would come later. For now, joy and relief gushed in to replace anxiety and despair. I felt comforted and encouraged, knowing that the words my parents had spoken that day—"Bobby, you're going to be okay"—were true.

Bodily reactions to the infusion of chemical agents

tell only half of the story. Visits to the IV center also trigger mental reactions. The sight of all those people hooked up to IVs, taking chemicals into their bodies they know will cause them to feel awful, spotlights the stakes of this struggle to survive. The situation feels grim, and humor is notably absent. I brought a bouquet one morning to add some color and cheer. The charge nurse took it to another wing, "because so many of the patients on chemo are hypersensitive to smells."

I resented the aura of depression and despair in the room. I needed some humor to lighten things up, so I asked Carolyn, my firstborn who had a few pet goats, to harvest a baggie of goat pellets.

"What are you going to do with that, Daddy?"

"I'm going to have some fun. Along with the chemo, I'm taking some medicine that they originally gave to goats to prevent worms. But coincidentally, they found that no animal taking this medicine ever developed colon cancer."

I took the packet of goat poop to my next visit with Dr. Crook. The nurse checked my vitals, made eye contact, and asked, "How are you doing?"

"I'm doing better now that I can eat," I replied, "but one thing bothers me."

She moved her stool closer and said, "What's that?"

I reached into my pocket and pulled out the pellets.

She laughed so hard she nearly fell off her stool. "You've got to show the doctor," she said.

"I plan to."

A few minutes later, Dr. Crook rapped on the door and entered the room.

"Hi, Bob,' he said, looking at the charts. "I see your numbers are continuing to improve; how are you doing?"

"I'm doing better now that I can eat, thanks to the Heavenly Pink, but one thing worries me."

"What's that?"

I pulled out the pellets.

His jaw dropped. He sat there and said nothing. When the silence grew too awkward, I said, "Just kidding."

Then he laughed and said, "Thank goodness. At first, when I saw those pellets, I thought, *What have I done to this man?*"

Reflecting on this event, the injection of humor did us all good; just what the doctor and the rest of us needed.

This moment anchored a turning point in my life, the beginning of a journey from disease and death to wellness and vitality, an act of grace in time of need. Ever since, I wake up saying, "Thank you, God, for giving me another day of life." It's such a precious gift. Maybe that's why we call it the present. Over forty-six years, that's 333 million breaths that I might never have taken.

Chapter 17

Transformation

....

F unny how certain events become turning points, dividing our lives into what happened before that moment and what came after. No matter how we long for the past, it is over, and it won't return. We can, and often do, ask why. I did, and I kept on asking why. I raised that question longer than was good for me. One day I had an aha experience: There was no answer to why. I never got one, and nobody I know ever did. I learned to ask a different question: What now? Now that this has happened, what can I do? Answers came. *I can be thankful I'm alive. God healed me, there was no evidence of disease in my body. I didn't die. God spared me.* These miracles of healing and life raised another question: What did God keep me around to do? For what purpose did God spare me?

What is the proper response to grace? How do you respond to being spared? You realize that you have nothing to do with it, that it was God's grace. Life is precious, and I received more when I thought it was over. At first, I said thank you. Then I felt like doing more. I sent up a trial balloon: a flyer announcing Divorce Care, a series of meetings to support those going through divorce. It was a test. I was divorced, and many friends were going through the emptiness of living alone. To my surprise, we got twenty-three responses. So I decided to start a group. We announced that the group would meet at church on Wednesday evenings at seven. I made an agreement with God that as long as people came, I would be there for them. The group changed when I learned about the Divorce Care curriculum, a transition we made without a hitch. The group met faithfully every Wednesday for twenty-two years. I only missed one meeting. Although I led it by myself for most of those years, all the time I was praying for someone to help. During the last five years, I was joined by Harriet Heibel. She was a welcome addition to the group, which was enriched by her presence.

I had the feeling that I was feeding Christ's sheep. When Jesus asked the Apostle Peter if he loved him, and Peter replied, "Yes," Jesus commanded, "Feed my sheep." Peter had betrayed the Lord at a most critical time. He needed to be forgiven and provided a job to do.

Christ forgave Peter and put him to work feeding his sheep. I felt I was doing that.

As far as we know, the universe is running down. In about six billion years, the sun will flame out, and life as we know it will cease to exist. Human beings have a lifespan of less than a hundred years. We're running down too. It's called entropy, running out of energy. Sometimes disease will intervene and shorten life. It has happened to our friends and loved ones, and we grieve those losses. How about this: Sometimes healing intervenes, entropy pauses, and life goes on. A life is spared. Is that not a cause for celebration? Especially if it's your life. I think of bowling. In the final frames, if I make a spare, I can keep bowling. A spare gives me some time I didn't think I was going to have. I'm living out those bonus years.

A new question comes up: Why am I here? What is my purpose in life? What does God want me to do? When I was in graduate school, the seminary offered a Templeton Prize for memorizing the Westminster Shorter Catechism; 125 questions for 125 bucks. Money was short in graduate school, so I was all in. The first question stayed with me: "What is the chief end of man?" Answer: "The chief end of man is to glorify God and enjoy God forever." Many years later, I understand more fully what that saying means. One of my longtime friends enjoys golf and has played most of the prestigious courses around the world. After retiring, he was able to play even more until his wife's health deteriorated, and he became her caregiver. He hired people from outside to help with parts of the daily routine, but there were some things she didn't want anyone but her husband to do. He has been her caregiver now for several years. He plays golf once a week with his friends, and at the end of eighteen holes, he's exhausted. He arrives home with an empty tank and no more gas to fix supper. I devised a plan and asked two of my friends to help me.

Each of us would prepare six servings of our favorite soup and put it in containers—six cartons each of potato leek, hamburger minestrone, and chicken curry soup. I called ahead so they'd be at home to receive it. When my friend came to the door and saw the box I was carrying, a smile as big as a Halloween jack-o'-lantern covered his face. Joy gushed up in me like water from an artesian well. I expected his happiness. My own pleasure surprised me. I learned that when I do loving acts of kindness to God's sheep, that makes God happy, and God sends me joy.

In my younger days, I was chained to dissociation. Early abuse trained me to go away as a strategy for survival. I survived the trauma of frequent enemas by my parents and molestation by an uncle by going away, dissociating myself from what was being done to my body. When colon cancer showed up in 1993, our twins were six months old. A voice inside my head was screaming, *You've got to get out of here!* That had been my pattern, to flee. When the going got tough, I went away.

This time I made the choice to stay. Deep inside I wanted to change, to learn to do things differently. The caterpillar wanted to go away, but a new behavior was being born. Grace was forming a new creature. I chose to stay, and I've reaffirmed that choice a thousand times. It's the best decision I have ever made. In June, Leslie and I celebrated our thirty-fourth anniversary. Grace provided a new empowerment. A butterfly was born.

What impact did my encounter with grace have on my life? After being spared, how was I different?

My metamorphosis happened in two stages. The initial changes occurred in 1977 after I recovered from melanoma. I drove purposefully to the Department of Motor Vehicles and applied for a personalized license plate. Instead of random numbers and letters, it said "BE-1SELF" to proclaim publicly a new awareness that

I had been born not to please others but to share my gifts. It highlighted a shift from taking care of other people to self-care. Being a caretaker and neglecting myself had left me depleted and resentful. This led me to a time of saying, "*No!*" I remember making a decision to say no to anything the church asked me to do for a year. I was learning that self-care is not selfish and, paradoxically, fills my cup, providing me more to share with others.

Self-care began with awareness and a question: What do *I* want? Mindfulness informed it. What color socks do I want to wear today? Brown or blue, or one of each, or none at all. Knowing I had choices empowered me.

Melanoma became my mentor. What did I need to learn? So far, I had been snorkeling, enjoying the view from the surface. Melanoma offered an invitation to dive deeper, to explore the unknown and make it known. SCUBA gear is needed to go deeper. This trip must be intentional. You don't float down to sixty feet below the surface. If you want to be there, you must descend to get there and adjust your buoyancy to stay there.

Exploring the deeper places of your soul requires intention too. Curiosity can help you overcome the fear of what you might discover. You will need to learn to be comfortable with silence, at peace inside your skin and in your own company. Learning to listen for the still, small voice will also help. Writers and other creatives know it's in this space that the muse speaks. An admirer once asked Leonard Cohen where he found his poetry and the lyrics for his songs. "If I knew that, I'd go there more often," he replied. Ideas seem to come out of the blue, often during our quiet times.

The most dramatic change was an attitude of gratitude. My point of view shifted from a belief that all my

blessings were the result of my hard work to an acknowledgment that they were unmerited expressions of God's
grace. Starting with life itself, I had nothing to do with
being born. I began to know more deeply how precious
life is, that it's a gift from the creator, and it deserves a
"thank you." Why should God continue to bless us when
we haven't said thank you for what we have?

Fifteen years later, a sigmoid resection triggered more
transformation. I bought a spiral notebook and printed
"My Gratitude Journal" on the cover with a black
Sharpie. Early each morning, I wrote down what I was
grateful for: life, health, vocation, food, rest, and children.
God had given so much that I had taken for granted.

Epilogue

I'm still learning that there's more. On February 23 of this year, I suffered a stroke. I was working on this book when it happened. I developed aphasia and I thought it was all over. The book was put on hold. I couldn't speak or write. Strokes are hemispheric. If they occur in the left hemisphere of the brain, they affect the right side of the body. Mine was left-sided. I couldn't speak or do much with my right side. I couldn't access the words I knew. Speaking was difficult because I didn't have words. I got a program from the speech therapist that kept pairing words so they wouldn't get lost.

Taking a shower is a new experience; an occupational therapist taught me how to do it when I couldn't use my right leg. She showed me how to be safe, especially getting in and out of the shower. And how to get dressed afterward when my right side didn't want to move. The physical therapist taught me how to walk again and how to regain my balance, telling me, "Much of it will come back. It's important to keep trying." I believed her, and it's true. Much of my speech is coming back as I practice talking. I am walking a mile when I initially couldn't go ten feet. I'm starting to get back to my computer. That's more of a challenge. Everything is different. When I was using the computer, the operating system was Windows 10 but now it is Windows 11. I can no longer use a regular mouse because I can't separate my fingers to activate it. I have an ergonomic joystick with my thumb moving side to side to activate the left and right clicks. It's been a lesson in patience.

The first thing I noticed as I recovered from the stroke was a supreme appreciation of little things. Like an empty urinal. It doesn't seem like much, but it's huge. Leslie emptied it, quietly doing what was needed. It's angel's work, an endless task but necessary, saving me from getting up in the middle of the night.

Then I got mobile. I could walk with a walker, and Leslie took me to acupuncture. Her doctor, Lana, came out on the sidewalk to greet me and welcomed me into her office. It happened she had spent years working with stoke victims at the Highland Hospital in Oakland. She helped me up on the table and made me comfortable. At first, I only felt like crying, and that was okay with her. I was unable to talk. I was feeling a lot of gratitude, but the words wouldn't come. So I just lay there sobbing and shaking, thankful for her ministrations. She said, "Some people just come to cry." The first few sessions were wordless. Gradually the words showed up, and I could express my thanks.

I'm grateful for my children who support me and visit me. I'm grateful for people who gave me a ride to church and back so I could attend Leslie's concert. I'm grateful for people who made meals and delivered them to our home. I'm grateful for the couple who invited us to have dinner with them at their home. That was my first outing. We enjoyed a gluten-free, low-sodium meal in their beautiful back yard. Shrimp cocktail, swordfish, and salad followed by fresh strawberries and homemade chocolate cookies.

ONCE AGAIN, GOD'S GRACE, my hard work, and loving help from others are allowing me to pick up where I left off, enjoying life and serving others.

Appendix

The Role of Stress in the Onset of Cancers

A t times I wondered what caused people to get cancer. Why do some people get it and others don't? Is there a genetic component? Do diet and exercise help prevent cancer? Or, once you have it, do they play a part in recovery? I read everything I could lay my hands on in my quest to find answers to my questions. My then-wife, Lynn, found a book that proved helpful, *Getting Well Again: A Step-by-Step, Self-Help Guide to Overcoming Cancer for Patients and their Families* by O. Carl Simonton, MD, Stephanie Matthews-Simonton, and James Creighton. On the overleaf, Lynn had written in her distinctive hand: "To Bob with all my love."

The authors explore the influence of stress on the human body and the connection of stress to illness. What follows is a summary of the major themes of the research:

- High levels of emotional stress increase susceptibility to illness.

- Chronic stress results in a suppression of the immune system, which in turn creates increased susceptibility to illness, especially cancer.

- Emotional stress, which suppresses the immune system, also leads to hormonal imbalances. These imbalances could increase the production of abnormal cells at precisely the time the body is least capable of destroying them. (p. 51)

The Simontons studied the work of Doctors Holmes and Rahe to explore the link between stress and illness. Holmes and Rahe developed a rating scale so they could objectively measure the amount of stress or emotional upset present in a person's life. Their social adjustment rating scale (SARS) identified stressful events such as death of a spouse (100), divorce (73), retirement (45), and signing a mortgage (31) that people commonly encounter in their lives and ranked them according to the amount of stress each event produces. (pps. 44-45)

Using these objective measurements, "Homes and Rahe were able to predict illness with a high level of statistical accuracy. Forty-nine percent of the people who had accumulated scores of 300+ points within twelve months on the scale reported illness during the study period, while only 9 percent for those with scores below 200 reported illnesses during the same period." (pps. 45-46)

Acknowledgments

Although *writing* a book is a solitary experience, *publishing* a book is not. Like producing a play, it takes a cast of characters. I want to thank them here.

Brooke Warner and Linda Joy Myers, whose excitement about the memoir genre rubbed off on me. Thanks, Brooke, for your constancy, encouragement, and consummate editorial skills. Thanks, Linda Joy, for your "keep writing" mantra, your group coaching sessions, and the memoirs you have written.

Ruth Stender, fellow author, and friend, whose intuitive insights blessed me along the way.

Tabitha Lahr, who created the cover and made what was inside it look great.

My daughter, Becky Garza, who laughed and cried with me as I wrote and gave me feedback about the parts that touched her heart and those that didn't.

Diana Stark, a member of my writing group whose poetry touches my heart, who asked me how I was changed in the writing process, prompting me to write the rest of my book with this question in mind.

Terry and Gary, the other two legs of our triad, thanks for listening and for your suggestions.

The Thursday Men's Breakfast Group who kept asking, "When will it be done?"

The people of Smith Patch—Mack and Ellen, Jerry, Stan, Royce, and Pat—who found it in their hearts to love me. I thought I was driving to Yoder to hunt mule deer and antelope all those years. Now I understand why my eyes filled with tears each year when I crossed the cattle guard, and the house came into view. They were tears of joy. I was coming home.

Carl Grant, who was an enlightened witness and spiritual guide through the journey.

Leslie, my wife, whom I treasure. You make our house a home and allow me space to write. Without you, this book would never have seen the light of day. Leslie also became my ghostwriter, finding previously written material, typing, emailing, and offering suggestions as I finished this book during recovery from a stroke—one more time I've been saved by grace.

Jordan Rosenfeld, the zoom classes, and the peer writing group that helped my writing get better.

My editor, Jennifer Caven, who waited between drafts as I recovered.

About the Author

B ob Finertie was born in the Garden State, New Jersey, and now lives three thousand miles west in the Golden State, California. He writes as a way of uncovering truth and giving voice to the unspoken broken inside. Some things are easier to write about than to talk about.

Here are a few of the author's favorites:

Favorite reads: Shakespeare and *Moby Dick.*
Favorite genres: Memoir and Poetry.
Favorite memoir: *Wild,* by Cheryl Strayed.
Favorite poets: Wendell Berry, David Whyte, and Amanda Gorman.
Favorite author: Frederick Buechner.
Favorite short story: "The Apple Tree," by John Galsworthy.
Bob's first memoir: *Be A Good Boy,* was published in 2018. *Grace in Time* is his second book.

Bob Lives in Walnut Creek with his wife, Leslie, and a Cavapoo named Copper. He enjoys hiking the open spaces and photography.

Connect with him at rwfinn@comcast.net.